D1368025

Liberation's Children

LIBERATION'S CHILDREN

......

Parents and Kids in a Postmodern Age

KAY S. HYMOWITZ

Ivan R. Dee
CHICAGO 2003

Most of the contents of this book appeared originally in *City Journal*, published by The Manhattan Institute.

Library of Congress Cataloging-in-Publication Data:
Hymowitz, Kay S., 1948–
    Liberation's children : parents and kids in a postmodern age / Kay S. Hymowitz.
       p. cm.
   Includes index.
   ISBN 1-56663-495-4 (alk. paper)
   1. Children—United States—Social conditions. 2. Parenting—United States. I. Title.
   HQ792.U5H959 2003
   305.23'0973—dc21   2003048574

To Paul

Contents

Introduction   xi

1 Fear and Loathing at the Day-Care Center   3

2 Survivor: The Manhattan Kindergarten   19

3 On *Sesame Street*, It's All Show   35

4 Raising Children for an Uncivil Society   54

5 Who Killed School Discipline?   73

6 Tweens: Ten Going on Sixteen   87

7 What's Wrong with the Kids?   108

8 The L Word: Love as Taboo   122

9 J. Crew U.   138

10 Ecstatic Capitalism's Brave New Work Ethic   150

11 The End of Herstory   170

Index   191

Acknowledgments

THANKS TO the Manhattan Institute, and especially to its president, Larry Mone. Thanks most of all to everyone at *City Journal*: to the three senior editors who worked with me on these essays, James Taranto, Gary Rosen, and Brian Anderson; and to Ed Craig, who saved me from any number of pop-culture blunders. And my deepest thanks to the magician editor, Myron Magnet, who always managed to read the argument deep inside my mind and to pull a shiny coin from my dull first draft.

K. S. H.

New York City
February 2003

Introduction

THESE ARE strange times to be growing up in America. A mere twenty years ago, who could have imagined a world where nine-month-olds use computers, ten-year-olds dress like Las Vegas showgirls, and high schoolers pass through halls with armed guards? Tracing the life script of middle-class Americans, from infancy to the school years to college and into their twenties, when young adults begin their careers and marriages, the essays in this book try to make sense of all this strangeness, as experts rarely seem to do, and in particular to understand how the postmodern American culture that produced the strangeness addresses the child's search for meaning. It asks: How does America speak to youthful ideals and aspirations today? What are American children learning from adults about how to live a meaningful life?

Tens of millions of kids growing up in places like Chicago's Hyde Park neighborhood or Loudon County, Virginia, have unprecedented opportunities to realize their talents and tastes—through soccer leagues, drama clubs, swimming teams, through hundreds of television channels and high-speed Internet access, through city-size malls lavish with food, clothes, and electronic playthings. To an extent unknown in human history, they can choose their entertainment, their dress and food, their hobbies and studies, and as they grow older their colleges, their careers, their workplaces, their living arrangements—all the while feeling pretty sure that adults will nod in approval.

But the same forces that have liberated today's kids from want, settled life paths, and confining traditions have also "freed" them from the moral and spiritual guidance that has always come from parents, teachers, and the culture at large. The result is not that today's kids "have no values," as pundits often tell us. On the contrary: American children develop Victorian-size superegos dedicated to the command to realize themselves through work. They hear endless moralizing about the virtues of tolerance and open-mindedness. The problem is that these virtues, important as they are, cannot help the young person build a self. Unmoored from all inherited structures of meaning, they tell kids not to judge, but not what to believe. They tell them to embrace all, but not what matters. They tell them to choose, but not why or how. In short, liberation's children live in a culture that frees the mind and soul by emptying them.

The essays that make up *Liberation's Children* were written over a span of seven years—a period that saw the horrific events at Columbine, an economic boom and bust, rising public concern about school discipline, and the emergence of that new social animal, the "tween." Yet the themes they trace remain central to the tragicomedy that is American childhood today. *Liberation's Children* begins with infants and toddlers, the subject of the first four chapters. These are the kids we used to think of as preschoolers—though clearly it's time to retire *that* term. Preparing for the meritocratic struggle for success, today's children begin their education before they can talk. As Americans have redefined infancy as

Introduction

the use-it-or-lose-it years of brain development, education now begins in the day-care center, or "early learning environment," as it is sometimes called, where infants embark on what will be at least two decades of specialized training of their cerebellums. As "Survivor: The Manhattan Kindergarten" (Chapter 2) describes it, the early child-rearing practices of the wealthiest Manhattan elites, though rarely involving day care, are only a rarefied version of trends familiar to the denizens of the middle-class neighborhoods throughout the country. No longer depending on breeding and bloodlines to assure their progeny a proper place in society, Manhattan's cognitive elite—from dealmakers to media brass—begin building their children's resumés at birth, when they start angling to get their children coveted spots in the city's posh nursery schools, which will get them into the "Baby Ivy" private elementary schools, which will in turn lead them to the hallowed gates of Harvard or Princeton. By three, New York's child of privilege has a CEO-intensive schedule of French lessons and swimming and gymnastic classes, as well as tutoring sessions, from which he can decompress during his vacations in Aspen and safaris in Kenya—where, of course, he'll be learning how to ski or speak Swahili.

Yet in far too many respects this meritocratic industriousness fails to speak to the child's longing for meaning. The universally beloved PBS series *Sesame Street*, the subject of Chapter 3, is a subtle example of how with the best intentions Americans sacrifice a rich tradition of individual soulcraft on the altar of mere brainpower. Hyped as offering the early learning experiences and cultural enrichment missing on the streets of Harlem and Chicago's West Side, *Sesame Street* in reality reduced education to bloodless, piecemeal skill development, enlivened only by dazzling media surfaces and sardonic humor. For all its reputation as manna for children, *Sesame Street* mocks much about childhood—its fairy tales, its love of adventure and wonder, its ignorance of the marketplace. In this way the show, first broadcast in 1969, signaled the profound change in childhood—now epitomized by the day-care center—that liberated the child to become an autonomous actor but removed the enriching sources of selfhood. Celebrating the media-savvy hipster over the clueless innocent, and reducing learning to technical skill training, *Sesame Street* introduced the postmodern child who is too hip, too on track to spend his time "doing nothing" listening to stories, pretending, or playing with anything other than "learning toys."

Anxious worrying about brain synapses and neural circuitry, gross motor and prereading skills also tends to underplay the other major task of the early years around which cultures have always organized themselves: introducing the young to mores and manners. It's as if Americans have concluded that while cognitive development should require parents to become neurology specialists—not to mention tycoons able to afford baroque music tapes, skill-enhancement toys, language classes, and maze tutors—social and moral development could come on the cheap. You can't read much these days about the delicate and deeply intimate task of instilling a bourgeois conscience in the young. Instead day-care advocates assure us that young children are getting what they need as long as they enjoy "positive caretaking behaviors" from preschool teachers who will cheerfully wave goodbye as the graduate moves from the infant room to the toddler room.

As Chapter 4 shows, popular advice givers have also added to the impression that socializing Megan and Daniel—bringing them into a preexisting community with shared

Introduction

meanings and values—barely requires adult attention. They have created a picture of a sensible, self-regulating child and a wholly improbable vision of the work that families do to socialize children. Look carefully at some of our most influential experts—Dr. Spock (still selling after all these years), Penelope Leach, the *What to Expect* series of advice books—and you will learn to your amazement that, if left to their own devices, young children will become toilet trained, give up the breast and the bottle, eat their broccoli, and say please and thank you. The cruel egotism of the terrible twos, the willful fours, rebellious adolescence? Not to worry. These are passing stages that kids will grow out of on their own, a notion that would bring a bitter smile to the faces of the teachers, coaches, and salespeople forced to endure the drearily long "stages" of other people's little darlings.

Chapter 5 traces how, in the name of liberation, the schools too leave children wanting. Over time the courts have vastly increased individual student rights. But while these rights may protect kids from arbitrary authority, they also have had the effect of depriving them of the sorts of communities that support the developing personality. Bureaucracies fearful of expensive and disruptive lawsuits rely on legalistic discipline codes, therapeutic programs, and zero-tolerance policies instead of the ordinary language that adults need to use in speaking to children. Educators lose the trust and respect of the young, who are by nature hungry for meaningful communities and for the guidance of adults who actually believe and know something important. As a result, we find ourselves with schools that range from service providers for the individual student and his "individual needs" to closely guarded detention centers.

It is when they reach the tween and teen years, the subject of Chapters 6 and 7, that children begin to show the worst effects of the adult silence that is the dark side of their liberation. Liberation's tween, those we used to call children between eight and twelve, are especially vulnerable in a world where adult convictions—at least those unrelated to achievement—seem to have wilted into vaguely held opinions. Too young to have a firm sense of themselves, yet old enough to have some independence, tweens turn away from the hesitant adults in their lives to a media only too happy to tell them the rules. Encouraged by *CosmoGIRL* magazine and MTV to display their hip knowingness through their Britneyfied clothes and Follow Me Boy body oil, tweens are ready to start dating by fourth grade; by middle school they are learning the how-tos of oral sex. It shouldn't surprise us that, as they get older, some abandoned tweens sink into a pleasureless and self-destructive nihilism. In Rockdale County, Georgia, a McMansion-filled Atlanta suburb, late-afternoon and nighttime orgies led to a syphilis outbreak that earned the attention of *Frontline* producers.

By just about every known social science measure, kids in suburbs like Rockdale ought to have been thriving. Their parents are "caring"; they have "good relationships" with their teachers. Yet though the people of Rockdale love their kids, they do not know how to transmit to them a world of convincing values or a vision of what life is about. The *Frontline* producers and the experts they interviewed, seeking to explain why a fourteen-year-old would have sex with fifty boys, concluded that Rockdale adults and teens had a communication problem. "Don't they see? Don't they see it's *them*? They don't talk to their children!" exclaimed a Rockdale minister to a public health official during a community meeting about the syphilis outbreak. But this explanation fails to consider the obvious: even if parents and teachers talk from dawn to *Letterman*, they may have nothing to say.

Introduction

Leaving the souls of kids like these all the hungrier is the demystification of sex and love or, as the title of Chapter 8 puts it, "The L Word." Sexual liberation was supposed to release the bodies of the young from the chains of taboo, secrecy, and religion. Yet this liberation also had the effect of hollowing out the soul's resources, as the desiring individual was reduced to his well-groomed body parts. In their sexuality education classes (abstinence education programs, which became more widespread after this essay was written, are sometimes another matter), kids hear nothing of love. They learn to think of sex as a friendly meeting of free, rational, autonomous selves, whose only complication is its potential health risk. Also fueling the cultural project of demystification has been the feminist ideal of the independent woman who can "explore her sexuality," leaving her emotions free to attach themselves to a career more gratifying than any male.

All this flight from passion gets its pictorial and musical accompaniment from a popular culture that glamorizes what the historian Peter Stearns has dubbed "American cool," an emotional style of tough, don't-need-nobody individualism. Indeed, cool detachment is a requirement of the American life script. The six-month-old must learn to separate calmly from his briefcase-toting mother (who is said to suffer not from the wrenching pangs of love, but only "guilt"). And when he's old enough (say, twelve?), he "hooks up" in one-night stands, the perfect way for him to "explore his sexuality" without any messy emotions that might interfere with his debate club's travels.

It is in college that kids get their highest education in the vacancy that their culture has gift-wrapped as freedom. Over the past thirty years, as postmodernism laid waste to the idea of "privileged" knowledge, the J. Crew University, as Chapter 9 calls it, has given up on a core curriculum and all but disposed of requirements, because no one in postmodern America, not even a college president, believes that he should say what liberation's children should know. Colleges, the prospective student learns from their eerily uniform promotional literature, want not to explain the cultural inheritance that led students to become who they are but to uphold "flexibility, openness, individual freedom." It's a strange irony: though permeated by postmodern thinking, which seeks to smash the "hegemony" of Western culture, our universities bolster the contemporary definition of true liberation as the individual floating outside cultural and moral traditions—a thoroughly American myth patched up out of Western ideas.

On reaching adulthood the middle-class American—detached from the past, emotionally cool, morally open, and dressed and primped for success—is well prepared to join the church of ecstatic capitalism, the subject of Chapter 10. At one time people associated work with routine, drudgery, and the man in the grey flannel suit; it was home and private life that allowed people to be their natural or authentic selves. But as the ethos of achievement swamped other cultural values, work seemed to offer the sort of meaning missing elsewhere in middle-class America. During the boom years of the 1990s, ecstatic capitalism promised—and has the potential to promise again in better times—that work would satisfy many of our most basic psychic needs and spiritual longings, for adventure, play, community, and even family. By the end of the twentieth century, as daughters who had been taken to work entered an exuberant economy, everyone—women, men, even children and babies in a manner of speaking—went to work.

Yet as my final chapter, "The End of Herstory," emphasizes once again, human aspiration will not be satisfied by a dedication only to work and individual achievement. Under the tutelage of their feminist mothers and teachers, today's young women grew up learning that their femininity and urge for children were a social construct; it was career that was central to their identity. They're not buying it. Though grateful to feminism's success in expanding their horizons, they are skeptical of its more radical attempts to make love taboo and to mythologize the pleasures of individual achievement. Ironically, this generation is not sold on the idea that children benefit from long hours of day care, even of the highest quality, though this has been an article of faith for their feminist elders and for early-education advocates. Having had firsthand experience with postmodern liberation, the daughters of feminism are less tempted by its assurances. They certainly know that freedom from permanent bonds—especially the most primal of all, that between mother and child—is not what it was cracked up to be.

The question now is: Will they reject the other false promises of postmodern culture that are the subject of *Liberation's Children*?

Liberation's Children

1

Fear and Loathing at the Day-Care Center

A few years ago I visited a Houston day-care center called Crème de la Crème. Experts define quality day care as clean and well-equipped centers, with sensitive, well-trained staff—but *this*, as its snooty name boasts, was to quality day care what the Plaza is to Motel 6. Past a lounge filled with overstuffed sofas, children walk into a Disneyland village of Victorian gingerbread storefronts, housing classrooms for Spanish and computer, a "Bibliothèque," and a shop selling Crème accessories. A bridge spanning a goldfish pond leads to a music room, a movement room, and a small library of curriculum guides for the professionally trained and unusually committed caretakers. Older kids can record themselves as they play-act at KREM-TV, the establishment's media center. Outside, along with the usual swings and slides, I saw a "Tyke Garage" crowded with pricey tricycles, and an elaborate shallow water park, with a sandy "beach" shaded by tropical plantings. Staggeringly lavish, this royal pleasure dome seemed to bespeak a child-centeredness that only the world's richest country could afford to build or even dream up. Only one sight seemed out of place: inside the door marked "Bébés, 0–12 Mois," were thirty cribs lined up in three rows of ten.

Not so long ago, the sight of thirty cribs, even supposing them tucked in with three-hundred-count sheets, evoked gloomy associations of hospitals and orphanages. But for the past three decades, day-care centers have become the cheerful setting of a new life script for American women. Shortly after women have their babies, the script goes, they head brightly back to work. Just as brightly, their babies head off to quality day-care centers, where professionally trained caregivers nurture them. The result is fulfillment for everybody: women find new satisfactions in work while achieving economic equality; young children thrive even more than they would under the care of their noncredentialed mothers. As the having-it-all script gained a following, though, certain chinks appeared: for one thing, a lot of women eagerly following its scenario reported suffering from feelings that seemed like . . . guilt. But it was always assumed that a high-quality center like Crème de la Crème would solve this problem, guaranteeing peace of mind for women and success for their children.

Or at least it seemed so until April 2001. That was when researchers from the National Institute of Child Health and Development (NICHD) released findings showing a link between long hours of nonmaternal care for young children and aggressive behavior. Though this was not the first time research had raised questions about whether day care might be associated with problem behavior, it was the first time that a large, longitudinal, government-sponsored, and highly publicized study had done so.

That didn't stop most opinion makers, including some of the study investigators themselves, from insisting that the findings were just not so: the research didn't prove cause and effect; it was inconclusive; people just didn't understand it. Furthermore, as far as they were concerned, even findings as carefully reviewed as these clearly were beside the point: after all, institutionalized care is now an established fact of contemporary life, and the only question worth considering is how to make it better. "Our job isn't to dissuade mothers from using child care by sending up these horror stories," the influential psychologist Edward Zigler, a Head Start founder, told the *Christian Science Monitor* in an extraordinary admission. "Our real task is to do a public education campaign with parents to get quality care."

Yet the profound question of how we rear the young will—and should—always be an open one, no matter how many experts declare it off-limits. And the truth is, the recent findings raise important questions about the choices young men and women face today. In a nutshell, the results indicate that the having-it-all script got some things wrong. Though promising fuller lives, it relied on an unrealistic, bloodless vision of both women and children, one that underestimated the passions of new mothers and minimized the complexity of socializing the young in an individualistic society. On close examination it seems that the script has not expanded the range of human possibility so much as it has demoted the values of love and interdependence associated with the home and family life, in favor of those values embodied in both the workplace and the day-care center: temporary relationships and individual achievement.

The day-care advocates, feminists, researchers, and sympathetic journalists who write the having-it-all script have always had one major public-relations problem: reassuring people that long hours away from mothers would not harm young children. For a long time this had been a surprisingly easy sell, what with study results showing that day care had no negative effect on infants' trust in their mothers, and that three-year-olds in high-quality day care had better language skills than their peers. Yes, other research suggested potential problems, but it was ambiguous or hidden away in obscure journals.

But when Jay Belsky, one of the two dozen or so researchers involved in the NICHD study, announced some of the 2001 findings at a press conference, it looked as if these reassurances were about to go up in smoke. The more hours children have been in the care of someone other than their mothers, Belsky stated, the more likely caregivers were to describe them, both at fifty-four months and at kindergarten age, as "aggressive"—a term covering a range of behavior from "demands a lot of attention" through "gets in lots of fights" all the way up to "cruelty." Whereas only 6 percent of the children in nonmaternal care for less than ten hours a week were described as aggressive, 10 percent of children between ten and twenty-nine hours were so rated and 17 percent of those children in care for more than thirty hours. This increased risk of aggression, Belsky went on, cannot be chalked up to maternal depression, poverty, or poor-quality day care, all ways to explain away such findings in previous research; this study controls for all of these.

Asked by someone to expand on the implications of the findings, Belsky, who had been one of the very few psychologists in the field previously to have expressed serious doubts about the effects of long hours of day care, responded: "If more time in all sorts of [day-care] arrangements is predicting disconcerting outcomes, then if you want to reduce the probability of those outcomes, you reduce the time in care. Extend parental leave and part-time work."

Belsky could be accused of jumping the gun—all of the NICHD's day-care research is observational and, strictly speaking, can't lead to conclusions about cause and effect or to recommendations about policy—but his proposals about what to do weren't all that radical. After all, though mainstream feminists generally emphasize "full workplace equality," advocating quality day care so that Mom and Dad can work equally hard, unhindered by Junior, a sizable group of women have also been making a plea for the parental leave and flexible work hours Belsky recommends. No matter. Committed to the proposition that there can be no middle ground between a wholehearted embrace of the all-day institutionalization of infants and toddlers and the fetishizing of motherhood in the style of the 1950s, feminists have greeted any suggestion that young children might suffer from long hours away from their mothers the way they'd greet a Taliban pronouncement that women would no longer be allowed to drive or exchange money. In the *Los Angeles Times*, Peggy Orenstein blasted Belsky's comments as "a 1950s-style attack." Even Belsky's co-researchers were furious. His behavior was "completely unprofessional," colleague Sarah Friedman told the on-line magazine *Salon*. "I know he differs from the group," she continued remarkably. "But . . . I thought that, since he was invited to represent the story, he would represent the party line."

"Party line" is an apt term. Day-care researchers may be scientists by training, but they look more like professional advocates in their efforts to sugarcoat the effects of day care on children and so to smooth the way to the workplace for young mothers. Consider the way NICHD tried to spin its big news in 1997. It reported two major findings that year: first, children in high-quality care showed slightly larger cognitive and linguistic gains than children in poor-quality care. Second, the more time children were in day care, the less affection they showed to their mothers at thirty-six months, and likewise the less sensitive their mothers were toward them. By the time the findings were massaged into a press release, they had been creatively transformed into a toast to quality day care: "New research . . . indicates that the quality of child care for very young children does matter for their cognitive development and their use of language. . . . In addition, quality child care in the early years . . . can also lead to better mother-child interaction, the study finds." Only pages later did the press release mention—quickly and dismissively—the more negative findings: "Researchers found that the amount of nonmaternal child care was weakly associated with less sensitive and engaged mother-child interaction."

The press happily colluded with the NICHD in headlining the good news for having-it-all script-lovers. "THE KIDS ARE ALL RIGHT," *Time* crowed. "DAY CARE STUDY OFFERS REASSURANCE TO WORKING PARENTS," the *Washington Post* announced. "GOOD DAY CARE FOUND TO AID COGNITIVE SKILLS OF CHILDREN" went the emollient headline in the *New York Times*. "These are heartwarming findings," Sarah Friedman—evidently satisfied that all of this toed the party line—told *USA Today*.

The press obliged no less readily when investigators tried to minimize the 2001 findings, showing bad news for day care. Reporters sought out interviews with the most skeptical "experts" and listed the reasons not to take it all very seriously—something few of them had bothered to do in 1997. No one seemed to notice that researchers all but admitted that they had looked for ways to make the 2001 findings go away. "When you come out with a finding that is negative and scary, you want to make sure you've done every possible analysis," NICHD researcher Alison Clarke-Stewart was quoted as saying. "There's more caution in the group in drawing implications that might be worrisome to parents," agreed her colleague Robert Pianta.

Fear and Loathing at the Day-Care Center

Reassuring the public that no harm would come to babies if their mothers left them for forty or fifty hours a week or more may have been the most challenging of the script-writers' tasks, but it was not the only one they faced. They also had to edit out any suggestion that women themselves might suffer from long hours away from their offspring. Gloria Steinem once said, approvingly, "We've become the men we wanted to marry." But some women found that, even so, they still had mothers' hearts.

Woe to those who got in the way of the attempt to deny maternal urges that might conflict with the script's fervent work ethic, however: as witness the reaction that greeted Felice Schwartz's 1989 *Harvard Business Review* article recommending that companies should have two tracks for women—one for those who were childless or inclined to hand most of their children's care over to someone else, and another (later dubbed the "Mommy Track") for those who wanted more time with their children. Those few mainstream feminists who didn't blast Schwartz were content to leave the dilemma she had pinpointed as a problem with no name. According to Ann Crittenden, author of the recent *The Price of Motherhood*, the editors of women's magazines like *Working Mother* and *New York Woman* told Schwartz: "It may be true what you're saying, but we just can't discuss these things in print."

Day-care researchers also didn't want to discuss any strong maternal feelings that might make the having-it-all script seem less than happily-ever-after. In fact, they implied, women who suffered from such feelings were immature and neurotic. In one 1997 paper, NICHD researchers went so far as to hint that putting an infant into a day-care center was a sign of a mother's psychological health. Mothers who went back to work when their babies were between three and five months, the paper reported, "scored higher on measures of extroversion and agreeableness" and—*quelle coincidence!*—were more likely to use center-based care. Those mothers who were reluctant to leave their babies, on the other hand, suffered from what the researchers condescendingly dubbed "separation anxiety" and tended to rely on relatives for care. Other experts, more commonly, reduced the emotional conflict between maternal love and career ambition to "guilt," the product of social demands unfairly foisted on women. "As a society," Barbara Willer of the National Association for the Education of Young Children told the *Washington Post* after the recent NICHD findings came out, "we've socialized women into feeling guilty." The experts' memo to mothers who don't want to leave their babies: Get over it.

But though mothers today might not want to return to life in the pre-script dark ages, clearly they don't want to get over their babies either. In *The Price of Motherhood*, Ann Crittenden gives voice to precisely the sorts of messy maternal longings that script advocates, in Orwellian fashion, had sought to turn into nonfeelings—feelings that are nothing like guilt and anxiety. An economics reporter for the *New York Times* and a Pulitzer Prize nominee, Crittenden should have been a poster woman for the having-it-all script. She was a success in a formerly male world; she and her husband had a comfortable income; she could have her baby, quality day care, and her glamorous job too. Instead she was "stricken with baby-hunger: a passionate almost physical longing for a child." And it didn't stop after her baby was born. "I fell hopelessly in love with this tiny new creature," she continues, "with an intensity that many mothers describe as 'besotted.'"

"Besotted" she must have been, because, in an almost incomprehensible betrayal of the script, she left her plum job at the *Times* to raise her child. Nor is she an anomaly. According to a 2000 *Newsweek* article entitled "Revisiting the Mommy Track," mothers between thirty-six and forty increasingly opt for the part-time work when their first child is born and often leave the labor force altogether with the second.

And other, even more conclusive data suggest that many women are similarly besotted. Of course, that's not the way these numbers usually sound. Almost every expert paper or news article you read about child care contains a sentence that goes something like this: "Close to 60 percent of mothers with children under a year are in the labor force, up from 31 percent in 1976." And that's true—as far as it goes. But the Bureau of Labor Statistics categorizes anyone who works for *an hour a week* as being "in the labor force"—and this fact alters the picture of maternal employment considerably. Among those 60 percent of mothers in the workforce are freelancers working at home while their babies nap. Among those 60 percent are also people like Susan Deritis, the publicity director of Mothers at Home, a support group for women who have elected to stay home with their children. She grabs a few hours to work every day—at home. According to the Bureau of Labor Statistics, she is a working mother, and, according to advocates, she is one of the reasons we should protect women from "worrisome" news about day care.

The real truth is that only 39 percent of mothers of children three and under, and only 43 percent of those with kids six and under, worked full-time in 2000. A Census Bureau pamphlet entitled "Who's Minding the Kids?" reports that 42 percent of kids under *five* have at least one parent neither employed nor in school. Another 19.4 percent of those children have a parent working only part-time.

What all this adds up to is the fact that somewhere over 60 percent of preschool children have at least one parent, the vast majority of them mothers, who either doesn't work or works only part-time. Given that close to one-third of all children in the United States are born to single mothers, who work at a considerably higher rate than married mothers, this is a particularly remarkable figure. It means that, despite the considerable financial sacrifice involved, a majority of parents of preschool-age children—and an even bigger majority of *married* mothers—are the primary caretakers of their preschool children. A 2000 survey from Public Agenda lends support to this picture: it found that 62 percent of respondents would like policies making it easier for one parent to stay home during a child's first few years, as opposed to only 30 percent who want policies improving the affordability and quality of day care.

Yet according to expert opinion—and government-sponsored expert opinion at that—findings in support of these views and in support of mothers who act on them are deemed "worrisome." The only welcome results are those that pave the path to the workplace. A Marxist surveying all this from the purgatory of defunct ideas might accuse the experts not of protecting women from disturbing information but of being tools of the corporate state attempting to expand and pacify the labor force.

But something very different is going on for today's followers of the having-it-all script. They are not dupes of market forces, and, unlike the original scriptwriters themselves, they're unlikely to be feminists. They are, instead, eager devotees of the contemporary creed of ecstatic capitalism. After years of taking A.P. courses and music lessons, listening to girl-power pep talks, and watching perfectly buffed and coiffed television-drama lawyers, they have learned to take for granted that job achievement is the primary arena for glamour, self-expression, and self-fulfillment. Of course, they expect to marry and have children, but they expect to consign them to a secondary role in the drama of life. After all, unlike dreary motherhood and housewifery, work for these young achievers promises public recognition, meaningful activity, creativity—maybe even adventure. Why, the workplace could even offer the camaraderie and friendships born out of intense devotion to a mutual cause, as on *ER*!

But as the Ann Crittendens of this world discover, there is an emptiness in the soul of woman under ecstatic capitalism. The office, with its ephemeral projects, water-cooler intimacies, and disposable employees, cannot satisfy the hunger for enduring connections, for the happiness that comes from the passionate love stirred by an utterly dependent being, for knowing and being known in ways only possible in the private space of family life, a hunger that neither thirty years of feminism nor ecstatic capitalism has been able to dispatch to a locked box marked Gender Stereotype.

The ideology of day care perfectly captures this revolution in values. Day-care devotees don't give much thought to young children's social and emotional growth, believing them to be relatively simple, even relatively unimportant, psychological matters. It is cognitive development, with its promise of future achievement, that really gets their juices flowing. In part their enthusiasm is understandable. It is easy to quantify and measure things like vocabulary and short-term memory; when it comes to the social and emotional development of a two-year-old, say, it's not even clear what scientists should be looking for, much less rating, outside of some gross maladjustment.

But children's cognitive development is at the heart of the having-it-all script chiefly because experts and parents have concluded that, in an increasingly meritocratic and work-obsessed society, brains win. Therefore infants and toddlers don't need "besotted" mothers—or fathers and grandmothers, for that matter—so much as they need good teachers. Seizing on highly publicized research in neuroscience, today's parents obsessively buy their babies Mozart CDs to improve spatial skills, French tapes to advance language development, crib mirrors to promote visual development, and textured teethers to stimulate the senses. For their part, experts willingly explain away research findings showing a link between long hours away from mother and childhood aggression while they noisily rejoice over findings showing that quality day care boosts verbal skills a tad.

No wonder that experts cheerfully observe that infant and toddler care is becoming increasingly like school. "Preschool is child care. Child care is preschool," as Danielle Ewen of the Children's Defense Fund told *Newsweek*. But day care doesn't provide education in the humanistic or civic sense; it is all business: it is school in the *vocational* sense. The point is to train babies, yes—for the workplace. "Good-quality child care is education," according to a pamphlet on day care from the Child Care Action Campaign, whose title—"Preparing the Workers of Tomorrow: A Report on Early Learning"—apparently is not a joke. It makes a certain kind of plodding sense. After all, you go to school, you're supposed to get smarter. You get smarter, you get a better job.

The problem with all this—aside from the absurdity of seeing a toothless infant batting at his crib gym as an executive-in-training—is that it slights the development of the young child's individual personality in the broadest sense. Yes, the problem-solving brain grows exponentially during early childhood, but so does the conscious self, the individual person with an identity that is larger than cognitive skill. Selfhood of the sort Americans have long prized implies a personal history—with its unique places and people—and a distinctive way of viewing the world that evolves in large measure out of experience within a family and a home with its own character. Moreover, the experience of selfhood finds continual reinforcement from family members who affirm the child as an individual like no other. Collective care, by its very definition, cannot do this.

On the kibbutz famously studied by the eminent child analyst Bruno Bettelheim in the 1960s, for instance, all infants were fed precisely the same amount, since "it was assumed their needs were entirely alike." In the seventies, sociologist Ruth Sidel found something similar in Chinese nurseries, where the group orientation was so deep that by the time children were toilet trained, they had learned to move their bowels in unison. Of course, this uniformity offends the Western sense of what constitutes a fully realized human being, and American experts try to define quality care, with requirements like low adult-child ratios and "sensitive, warm caregivers," in a way that would assure individualized treatment even within an institution. Surely this is to be preferred over synchronized bowel movements.

But in the final analysis, "quality" care is still a pale imitation of what young children can get from besotted families. Even if the professional caregiver "responds to vocalizations" or "places infant near where she can see other infants"—two items on the NICHD researchers' list of "positive caregiving behaviors"—she cannot represent a distinctive perspective or imprint her personality on the unformed child. Nor can she possibly have a deep commitment to—or love of—that child, with all his unique tics and tendencies. Not only does she have several other babies to care for at that moment; she knows that in short order each of them will be moving on to the pretoddler or toddler room to a new set of sensitive, warm, but ultimately replaceable, teacher-caregivers.

Most important in the current debate, the having-it-all script, with its veneration of workplace and cognitive achievement, seriously minimizes the emotional complexity of the civilizing process in an individualistic society. Families not only nurture the child's individual personality; they also teach the child how to moderate it. As today's child-development experts ignore, but as generations of psychologists understood, the child does not simply learn self-control the way he learns to develop his fine motor skills. He must internalize the moral requirements of his culture, make them part of his very nature and identity, so that they feel as natural as breathing.

Of course, there are any number of ways this can happen. In many premodern societies, children learned to obey society's rules because they feared the rod. In the kibbutz, according to Bettelheim, children behaved because they learned to identify closely with the peer group and didn't want to let it down. But most Western bourgeois societies, especially ours, discipline children through love, a huge psychic undertaking. Out of love, parents, particularly mothers, devote themselves to nurturing the child's individual talents, interests, and temperament. Meanwhile the child's desire to please the adored mother and his fear of losing her love when she disapproves of him make him want to behave as she wishes him to. This intense emotional stew has its dangers, but it has managed to cultivate individuals who can balance individual expressiveness with self-restraint. And it does suggest a reason why young children spending long hours away from their mothers might be more inclined to "get in lots of fights" and show "cruelty." They have not had the opportunity to develop with sufficient intensity the bonds that anchor the bourgeois conscience.

Though no one bothered to mention it during the 2001 NICHD fracas, experts have had evidence for a long time of something amiss in the having-it-all script's view of how children become socialized. Ever since developmental psychologists began studying the subject in the late 1960s, as the first wave of postwar mothers started flooding into the labor force, they have persistently glimpsed indications of some link between day care and behavior problems. Alison Clarke-Stewart, one of the NICHD investigators, in a 1993 book that is otherwise so rhapsodic that you come away wondering whether institutionalized care should be mandatory for all infants, nevertheless had to admit that there were substantial findings showing day-care kids to be "less polite, less agreeable, less respectful of others' rights, more irritable, more rebellious . . . more aggressive with their peers."

Clearly none of this means that day care is a training ground for the future Timothy McVeighs of America. Even the NICHD findings show only modest effects: children the study rated as more aggressive were still within the range of normal. Moreover, 17 percent of children in the general population are rated aggressive on the scale the researchers used, the same percentage as the kids in the longest hours of care. And for some underclass kids there's evidence that full-time day care may provide nurture lacking at home.

But the widespread, relentless, high-pressure effort to deny that findings like these have any significance—or to put a mendacious positive spin on them—springs not just from an unwillingness to hear bad news about day care but from the broader tendency of our era to trivialize the deep problem of the socialization of children, especially thorny in a culture always needing to guard against the excesses of individualism. "Is it possible that kids are born aggressive, defiant, raring to talk too much at the first opportunity? Is that a bad thing?" *Salon's* Jennifer Foote Sweeney wonders. "There's no evidence to suggest that an aggressive kindergartner will grow up to be a bully," chimes in an editorial in the *Philadelphia Inquirer*. "In fact, she might just become a CEO. . . . Also largely overlooked was the good news that children in high-quality day care are academically advanced. . . . Make that a smart, articulate CEO." As long as the child grows up to be a high-achiever—meaning, it seems, that she escapes the Mommy Track—is it really so important that she is obnoxious or even vaguely immoral? Success trumps character and civility any day.

All this confirms what philosophers have known since the time of Plato, of course: how we rear our children reflects the kind of society we are. And here the having-it-all script should give us pause. Its veneration of work and professional achievement over all other human goods pays insufficient attention to the well-being of children and the society they will inherit.

Our young mothers- and fathers-to-be face difficult choices, which they need to make with as much wisdom and understanding as possible. If the experts and the pundits would only let them.

[2001]

2

Survivor: The Manhattan Kindergarten

Mrs. G. recalls it as "the darkest year of my life." She cried all the time. She had trouble speaking in complete sentences. She lost fifteen pounds. One of her friends remembers fearing that the stylish blond mother of two, and owner of both an Upper East Side apartment and a Long Island beachfront home, was suicidal.

A child stricken with cancer? The collapse of her husband's business? The death of a beloved parent? Menopause? No, the darkest year of Mrs. G.'s life came the year her son was rejected from kindergarten.

It's hard to imagine writing such a sentence as anything other than a joke, but for members of New York's elite like Mrs. G., kindergarten is an intensely serious business, given the status anxiety that besets even—perhaps especially—the elites in a dizzyingly meritocratic society. Between a baby boom and an economic boom that sharpened competition, getting your child into one of New York City's select private schools has become a grueling, multi-year competition, with its own rules, code language, and intrigue. It's a mean competition, too—one that can turn sensible, mannerly, child-loving parents and educators into hard, calculating, and paranoid operators. (Almost everyone interviewed for this article insisted that she not be quoted by name and that all identifying characteristics be disguised. "I can't talk about it," one mother of twins announced, banging down the phone.)

That applying to kindergarten should become such a cut-throat business is doubtless an only-in-New-York phenomenon, intertwined with New Yorkers' considerable self-regard. If Mr. and Mrs. Big have made it here, then their children have to make it here too; they must "take their rightful places as leaders in the world of tomorrow," as the promotional literature from Chapin, one of the city's toniest girls' schools, puts it. Still, if this Park Avenue version of the game of *Survivor* is something of a cultural oddity, the attitude toward young children that it imposes is not. The pint-size contestants of the jungles of Gotham are merely the most striking example of a profound change in American sentiments about early childhood, as our meritocratic knowledge economy transforms toddlerhood from a mommy-and-me period of fantasy and free play to turbocharged years of resumé-building and networking.

The seventy-odd private schools in or near Manhattan are a varied lot, but with few exceptions they share one notable quality: age. They have the mystique of wood-paneled privilege that is hard to manufacture anew and that continues to radiate the glamour that makes even pop divas like Madonna aspire to Scottish castles and English nannies. Many of these schools are housed in fine, old Upper East Side buildings or ivy-covered campuses; students often wear uniforms, including blazers or kilts; they honor traditions like teas and

Founders' Days; they may even call teachers "Sir." History has given each of these institutions a unique character. Towne and Allen-Stevenson are small, traditional schools with a neighborhood tone; Little Red Schoolhouse and Trevor Day have a staunchly 1920s left-wing feel; Grace Church, Marymount, and Sacred Heart have proud religious affiliations.

But it is what Victoria Goldman, co-author of *The Manhattan Family Guide to Private Schools*, calls the Baby Ivies that are the million-dollar prize of this *Survivor* game. These are the *crème de la crème*, the Harvard, Yale, and Princeton of the K-12 set. Decades ago these schools could easily be divided into two broad categories. The coed, progressive schools—Dalton, Fieldston, Friends Seminary, Horace Mann, Riverdale, and St. Ann's—appealed to New York's artistic and intellectual elite. The unisex traditional schools—Buckley, Collegiate, St. Bernard's, and Trinity (now coed) for boys or Brearley, Chapin, Nightingale-Bamford, and Spence for girls—educated the children of the Protestant establishment, at least until adolescence, when many of the boys went on to board at Groton and Choate. (St. Bernard's and Buckley still go only to the ninth grade.) These days all the schools pride themselves on a progressive, multicultural curriculum that counts as today's conventional wisdom; you would be just as likely to find a first-grade "interdisciplinary project" on Eskimos at Collegiate as at Dalton, and a tenth-grade African-American literature course at Spence as at Fieldston. All of them "respect different learning styles." Yet despite the trendy veneer, the curricula remain fairly rigorous, and the schools still turn out graduates who know the difference between a Van Gogh and a Vermeer, speak French, and play decent tennis.

At one time, getting into these schools, even the Baby

Ivies, wasn't hard. Until the end of the hat-and-white-glove decade of the fifties, your child's school simply reflected the Natural Order of Things. She went to Spence, he went to St. Bernard's—or Dalton or Horace Mann if you were Jewish—in the same way that you belonged to Brick Church or Temple Emanu-El or that tulips bloomed on the central strip of Park Avenue in the spring. But by the sixties a burgeoning upper middle class of businessmen and professionals, many of them Jewish, began knocking on the doors of the clubby Protestant schools. At the same time the emerging vision of meritocracy that was leading Ivy League colleges to prize brains over breeding was filtering down to the city's private schools. At least when it came to their children's schooling, it was beginning to seem that the rich could no longer afford to be careless. As of 1968 *The New York Times Guide to New York City Private Schools* was reporting growing anxiety among Manhattan parents: "As a dinner party conversation, [private school] is beginning to replace such subjects as the shortage of apartments and household help." Rumor had it that Brearley was actually turning down the "academically below par" children of wealthy alumnae!

Still, between stagnant birthrates, economic downturns, and a stock-market crash, the competition to get into private school over the next several decades never went too far beyond genteel. The same could not be said of the nineties. Applications to private kindergarten increased by some 25 percent between the beginning and the end of the decade. One mother applying to Friends Seminary several years ago was told that the school had enough applicants to fill seven kindergartens. Between 1999 and 2001, some one hundred nursery schoolers failed to be admitted to *any* tony kindergarten.

To ensure that their children get in somewhere, parents

now apply to ten or even twelve schools, some of them in godforsaken Brooklyn. Brooklyn Friends saw a 35 percent increase in applicants in the late nineties, a significant number of them Manhattanites. Poly Prep, in other-side-of-the-tracks Bay Ridge (once best known as the location for the disco movie *Saturday Night Fever*), now boasts 25 percent of its student body from Manhattan, up from 5 percent only ten years ago. And "boasts" is the correct word: except for the eccentric and prestigious St. Ann's, Brooklyn schools are the Appalachian cousins of the Baby Ivies and take great pride in the number of their Manhattan applicants; they manage to let prospective parents hear about it on tours and in interviews.

So keen is the kindergarten competition that it has trickled down to the nursery schools. Manhattan parents have always banked on the assumption that getting their three-year-old into a "feeder" nursery that has traditionally sent its children on to the top-tier elementary schools would assure them of one of those coveted spots. In 2000, however, for the first time in anyone's memory, some of the city's most elite nursery schools saw families like Mrs. G.'s rejected from all their choices. This has only spread the *Survivor* frenzy to the city's elite nursery schools. Manhattan parents are now applying to six or seven nursery schools. Several years ago the 92nd Street YMHA, a school whose director, according to the parents' grapevine, has a way with Baby Ivy admissions people, held eight meetings for prospective parents, some of them packed with fifty families. The school had only twenty-five openings and applications from so many sisters of current students that they told the desperate masses, "If you're a girl, don't apply."

Just about everyone points to four reasons for this crush of ambitious tots. First, a record number of births nationwide—the "baby boom echo"—has hit densely populated New York especially hard. The city's public schools had the biggest jump in enrollment in 1997–1998 of any school system in the country; the Big Apple's comfortable private schools are part of the same trend. Also, more families with school-age children wanted to stay in New York, because (Reason Two), with lower crime rates and a less in-your-face street life, Gotham had become a more family-friendly town, and (Reason Three) the bustling economy meant that more people could afford private school—which is saying a good deal when kindergarten tuitions hover around $14,000. It used to be that families headed to Scarsdale or Chappaqua when their firstborn hit school age, but by the late nineties private schools were seeing plenty of three- and even four-child families. Finally, like colleges, private schools increasingly want to recruit a diverse student body. Jackie Pelzer, executive director of Early Steps, which guides neophyte minority parents through the application process, reports that last year she placed 125 children, by far the largest number since the organization was founded in 1986.

Add the diversity imperative to the number of children of alumni and siblings of current students, both of whom get preferential treatment in admissions, and what you have left is only a handful of openings. One Upper East Side nursery school director making her routine yearly phone call to discuss her applicant pool was told by the director of admissions at one top kindergarten: "We're only looking for diversity. We're not interested in your Caucasian kids."

But though no one likes to talk about it, there is more at work here than increased demand. The Darwinian struggle for a private kindergarten spot is also evidence of the triumph of the cognitive elitism that began in the sixties. The meritocracy has arrived at the playground. As a general rule, the more prestigious the private school, the more aggressively brainy the kids. To get your child into Collegiate or Horace Mann (a school where, legend has it, parents chanted, "Our SATs are higher than yours!" during a soccer game against Fieldston) is to confirm that he is one of the cognitive elect. "Old-money parents were not out to impress anyone; they just wanted to be with their own kind," explains Ronald Bazarini, author of *Boys: A Schoolmaster's Journal* and a teacher at St. Bernard's for twenty-five years before retiring some years ago. The new-money parents of today are a different matter. Their children's school reflects their most revered quality, their own intelligence. As a result, according to Barbara Root, director of admissions at Sacred Heart, the school becomes part of a "product orientation–measurable success: where you go to college, what kind of job you have."

Making things more loaded for today's parents is that other sources of identity and status have faded in significance. For Manhattan's hereditary ruling class, the private school was only one of many signifiers. For the educated elites who now dominate Manhattan, school, appropriately enough, dominates. "Private schools have replaced the church and country club," says Russell Pennoyer, a St. Bernard's alumnus who has served on its board and is the parent of three private-school children. "It's where you look for your social set." The authors of *The Manhattan Family Guide to Private Schools* quip that "The Headmaster's Circle," a select group of large donors at some schools, is "the 90's equivalent of The Social Register." One mother I interviewed described how her daughter's nursery school director gently suggested that the child would be happier at a "nurturing" (read: less academically high-pressure) school like Hewitt instead of Spence, the high-powered school she had hoped for. I asked another director about Hewitt. "I have plenty of families who would rather die than say their child goes to Hewitt," she sniffed. "It paints 'loser' on your forehead." In short, your child's perceived brainpower says a lot about who you are in New York City.

So, just how do admissions directors measure braininess in a *four*-year-old? Through an IQ test, the revised Wechsler Preschool and Primary Scale of Intelligence, required of all children applying to kindergarten in Manhattan private schools. Actually, people never call it an IQ test; they refer to it as the ERB, after the Educational Records Bureau that administers it. One Upper East Side nursery school director speculates that today many schools base 50 percent of their decision on IQ scores. "Now I hear all the time, 'He didn't do so well on his mazes [one of the tasks on the ERB].' You never heard that ten years ago. [At that time] I could have said to a director of admissions, 'We have a wonderful child,' and they would take another look. Now they say, 'No. I can see this dumpling is adorable, but his fine motor skills are a little weak.'"

Given the size of the stakes, parents go into full battle mode over the ERBs. They buy workbooks of mazes and shapes; they ask their child's nursery school to practice ERB-type tasks in class, which many of them do. Some families hire tutors, though they never call them that. When I asked one Upper East Side child psychologist if she knew of any children being tutored for the ERB, she said no—before proceeding to describe how she had placed her own child in a program "to develop his fine motor skills." Bellen Nicholson, a private tutor, recalls asking one of her clients if she could give her name as a recommendation. The woman refused: "I think this program is wonderful," she explained, "but this is my find. I will not share it." Actually, the unspoken rule is that you *never* allow anyone to know your child is being tutored. People don't schedule play dates for at least an hour after Nicholson leaves their home, to avoid the danger of a nanny-spy barging in on a session, partly because parents want their child to seem effortlessly brilliant, *sprezzatura* for the educated elites.

Aside from the ERBs, the schools also try to weed out the master race from the adorable dumplings by age. To be considered for kindergarten at most schools, a child must be five by either September 1 or October 1. But the simple truth is, older kids tend to know more than younger kids. Parents figured this out a while ago; they've been holding the applications of their late-summer babies back a year, hoping the child will have a better shot at impressing an interviewer. Now schools are joining them at this game; several of them have informed nursery school directors that they're not looking for young birthdays—meaning June, July, or August. Why? Simple, one nursery school director answers: "They're looking for bigger, better, stronger children."

To be fair, they're looking for bigger and better children because they believe that school is harder than it once was. Maggie Granados, head of admissions at Berkeley Carroll, a small, second-tier Brooklyn school, says that, because of more preschool and parental tutoring, she is seeing so many kindergartners who are strong readers that she is no more impressed than she used to be if a child could tie his shoes. "It's not their parents' kindergarten," Granados cautions.

The result is an admissions process that is not for the tenderhearted. Take this statement from one nursery school director: "I have one family this year with a son at a well-known coed school. They want a very competitive girls' school; they've limited themselves to the Ivy League. But the child is totally ordinary. She clung to her mother during one interview. (The Baby-Ivy-bound four-year-old is far too self-confident to demonstrate any separation anxiety or shyness.) Her ERBs are ordinary. She's not particularly verbal in class; she has no insightful comments after we read to her. . . . She's a darling, ordinary child who needs to go to Amherst, not Harvard. The father has come to see me ninety-eight times. 'I know this person on the board. I've heard you're really good at getting kids into good schools. I expect to be one of those families. You know how supportive I've been.' He gave me a modest check at the auction. This child will get in nowhere."

Of course, private schools, particularly in the early grades, can never be full-blooded meritocracies. For one thing, no one but the most hard-line test-crusader is willing to put *that* much stock in the score that a volatile four-year-old achieves on a seventy-five-minute assessment. And, more practically, private schools depend on parent and alumni money. Annual auctions and fund drives have allowed Dalton to add its top-floor sky-lit art studios with Manhattan views and Chapin to build its new gym, choral room, library/multimedia center, and black-box theater, as well as to renovate its greenhouse (from which it is traditional that each child applicant receives a plant). And a stream of contributions allows all the schools to maintain impressive endowments and substantial scholarship funds.

In addition, a certain polish and *je ne sais quoi* are a must. No small measure of the enormous anxiety among today's prospective kindergarten parents arises out of the recognition that the elite private schools retain a modicum of class snobbery. Depending on the school, applicants must—or can—provide reference letters from someone who supposedly knows the child. Parents scour their social horizon, looking for any dignitary or semi-dignitary, however distant or implausible. One of your firm's partners is on the board at Chapin; a friend of a friend knows Chuck Schumer. (One desperate mother admitted that when she and her husband heard my message on their answering machine asking for an interview, he looked at her and said: "Do you think she can help us get into private school?") School administrators roll their eyes at all of this, and it's clear that there's no longer any one right connection that will seal the deal. But the fact that admissions offices still pay any attention to these letters helps explain the odd combination of Old World manners mixed with knowledge-economy hustling and self-promotion that characterizes this game of *Survivor*.

Consider the social-climbing rituals associated with the early stages of the game: applying to nursery school. Even before their children are born, parents join prestige churches and synagogues that, in addition to exuding an old-money aura, are attached to nursery schools with a good record of private school admissions. "New Members" Sundays at places like Brick Church and All Souls Unitarian, both of them with highly regarded nurseries, are jammed with pregnant women and families with small children who have suddenly found religion. At nursery school interviews, wives obsess over what clothes they and their husbands should wear. They elbow their spouses who tell the wrong joke or yawn. And after these exercises in humiliation, they write thank-you notes. One mother of a two-and-a-half-year-old nursery school aspirant read me hers, composed over several hours, then edited and handwritten by her husband, who, the couple decided, has the better cursive (but not the better eye; the husband reduced his wife to sputtering rage when he inadvertently placed his completed letter, written on white Crane's stationery, in a cream-colored Crane's envelope).

Dear [director's name]:

We would like to thank you for a wonderfully informative tour of your school. We loved it! It was wonderful to see children so actively engaged in their play and their projects, specifically [describe specific project to avoid sounding like a form letter]. How lucky the children are to have the [name] School as their first formal educational experience. We would love for our daughter to have such an opportunity. We believe that she would thrive in such an atmosphere of enthusiastic learning and exploration.

Thank you very much for the opportunity to explore the [name] School.

Sincerely,
[Parents' names]

Does the right nursery school matter enough for all this? One unsuccessful private school parent-applicant thinks so. "My kid had been in day care," she scoffs. "He might as well have been on welfare."

Besides cultivating charm and connections, parents also try to give their toddler-applicants a little knowledge-economy polish through extracurricular—or, to be more exact, precurricular—activities. The aspiring Spence or Collegiate tot doesn't waste much time swinging on monkey bars at the playground. By fifteen months he has a busy schedule of four or five activities. One Upper East Side "feeder" nursery school director read me one applicant's Attachment A (Attachment B was a letter from a high-profile businessman whose child had gone to the school): Jodi's

Gym, Hands On (a music course), and various classes at Rhinelander Center, 92nd Street Y, and 74th Street Magic. It also lists (as does almost every other application she has received) the Upper East Side baby fad *du jour*, "Language for Tots," a foreign-language program for kids starting at six months.

The truth is, educators subtly encourage this sort of hyperstrategizing. In evaluating applications, a number of preschools secretly give letter grades to families. And it isn't just a father who doesn't show up for an interview or a mother arriving in jeans that leads to a C-minus. "Our admissions are driven by how easily or not we can place a child in kindergarten," admits another East Side nursery school director. "We do let the occasional lowbrow family in. But if the mom's loud and is wearing garish colors, has bleached hair—I don't mean highlighted—I've got to say to myself, 'Okay, nice family, terrific kid, but I'm not getting this mother past admissions at Collegiate.'" What's more, there are benefits to the hysteria. "A lot of my colleagues say, 'What can we do to alleviate this? It's out of control,'" the director continues. "But they take a certain glee that people will do just about anything to get their child into their school. The buzz validates that they are great schools." And this is just applying to nursery school!

Of course, the primary schools are equally guilty. Their admissions directors, wanting to burnish their institution's reputation for being a hot school, maneuver to ensure that all the families they accept actually sign contracts, and nursery school heads have been known to suffer their wrath when one of their families turns them down. Meanwhile, no matter how much parents research and prepare, many end up mystified by much of what goes on in the kindergarten *Survivor* game. One mother puzzled over why her son was rejected at the five schools that she applied to last year. She had gotten the letters from influential people, she and her husband had avoided any grave *faux pas* at their interview, and the child had evidently scored well. "He had great ERBs. Listen to the last line: 'A delightful child.' And on top of that, he interviewed well." Then she paused in a way few parents or educators had paused in the scores of interviews I'd had. "I can't believe I'm saying this about a four-year-old."

But then in a world scouting for "bigger, better, stronger children," people seem to be saying—and doing—all sorts of things about four-year-olds that they've never said and done before. The fate of affluent Manhattan toddlers and pre-schoolers may not rank high up there on the list of childhood tragedies, but it poses its own dangers. A high-powered, mer-itocratic culture pushes adults to begin building their chil-dren's resumés and expanding their networks even in the preschool years. Says Sacred Heart's Barbara Root: "There's no trust in letting things happen in their own time." A vet-eran educator at one of the elite girls' schools is struck with the exhausting pace of life for these young children. "They go to a matinee of *Amahl and the Night Visitors* and then a night performance of *The Nutcracker*, a week of vacation skiing in Colorado and the second week on a beach somewhere, play dates every free afternoon and sleepovers every weekend." Third-graders, she continues, have taken to carrying Filofax planners. First- and second-graders complain of what are clearly stress-related headaches and stomachaches. "'I'm flustered,' 'I'm hurried,' 'I'm stressed,' they say."

Nor is "parenting as product development," as William Doherty, a University of Minnesota sociologist calls it, unique to New York City. All over the Midwest, Doherty says, parents hold their children back from first grade in order to make them stronger when it's time to be on the high school hockey team. In one Minnesota town, until some parents balked, a team of four-year-olds held a weekly hockey practice the only time the rink was available—at 5 a.m. Nationwide the peer pressure on parents is intense. What parents wouldn't begin to doubt themselves when they hear that their three-year-old neighbor can count to twenty in three languages or that their four-year-old niece can surf the Internet, when their child spends his days finger painting and playing Darth Vader, and counts going to the zoo as his greatest adventure?

The bigger danger is that, as parents put so much of their energy into branding their child-products, achievement threatens to become the only means by which they know and judge their children. As a result, to the most ambitious parents, bright kids don't seem bright enough anymore. When parents receive less-than-dazzling ERB scores, the doubt begins to gnaw. "They have a child who is bright and funny, and suddenly they're wondering, 'Should we get tutoring?'" says one nursery school director. Tutor Bellen Nicholson recalls one mother who called her after a disappointing but hardly disastrous ERB score, crying: "Is something wrong with my child?"

High-scoring children face a different sort of problem. Parents who believe that their child is "brilliant"—and teachers nationwide will tell you that there are many of them who've never even been near an IQ test—often seem to conclude that they should be immune from ordinary social expectations. "If he can't pass the juice or look you in the eye, they say, 'Oh, he's bored,'" according to one experienced nursery school teacher. Why should one of the elect be bothered about table manners if cognitive ability, without virtue or civility, is the alpha and omega of human excellence?

Still, there are resisters. "I think it's nagging on people

that we live in a mad, mad world. These kids are rushing into a New York power life," says one mother of four-year-old twins, who, amazingly, don't even go to nursery school. "But why is it so important to be somewhere at 8:30 when you're three?" Another disgusted mother told the one private school where her son was wait-listed to just forget it—and put him into public school. "At first I thought, 'I'm a bad mother,'" she reports. "'I'm not giving him all the advantages I can. He's going to be pulling garment racks down Seventh Avenue.' That's crazy. He's in *kindergarten*."

What such resisters seem to grasp is that, especially in today's economy, there are many kinds of stories imaginable. A child goes to public school, discovers his talent at SUNY Purchase, and starts a successful consulting business. His rich cousin goes to Buckley and lands at Harvard Law before joining Cravath Swain, where he drowns his misery in Stolichnaya. Another child does well at Hewitt, graduates magna from Yale, but, wanting time for her children, takes a part-time job as a photographer at a small-town newspaper.

That's the thing about the wild ride of the American biography. It can be hard to guess the end from the beginning.

[2001]

3

On *Sesame Street,*
It's All Show

It would be hard to think of another modern institution that has touched as many children as *Sesame Street.* In Television-land, where shows have a shelf life as brief as that of a carton of eggs, this one is still going strong after more than a quarter-century. During that time it has been broadcast to more than 120 million children in 130 nations from Israel to Mozambique, making it—according to the Children's Television Workshop, the show's producer—"the largest single teacher of young children in the world." In the United States, *Sesame Street's* popularity is staggering; 77 percent of American preschool children from all areas, ethnic groups, and income levels watch the show once a week or more. In many locales they can take their pick of three or more broadcasts a day. "We're like the British Empire," one of the show's creators quipped presciently during the first season. "Someday the sun will never set on *Sesame Street.*"

Winner of fifty-eight Emmys, two Peabody Awards, and four Parents' Choice Awards, subject of retrospectives at the Smithsonian Institution and the Museum of Modern Art, *Sesame Street* is as revered as it is popular. From its earliest years, when U.S. Commissioner of Education Sidney Marland proclaimed the show "among the supreme revelations of my thirty years in education," to recently, when John Wright of the University of Kansas's Center for Research on the Influences of Television on Children recommended it as "part of a balanced breakfast," experts have pronounced the show "quality children's programming," a completely different breed from *Mighty Morphin Power Rangers*. Through its role as teacher of young children, and because of its much vaunted racial and ethnic sensitivity, it often serves as the national symbol of compassion, as in a memorable 1995 performance of Bert and Ernie, directed by Representative Nita Lowey, at a congressional hearing over funding for the Corporation for Public Broadcasting.

So it comes as some surprise when you actually sit down to watch this marvel. Don't expect a show that, like a good book, inspires children's developing emotional or moral life, that engages their imaginations, that piques their curiosity about the world or enriches their experiences of language. *Sesame Street* is an educational revelation, all right—the kind we've experienced so often recently in depressing reports about the declining verbal abilities of American students. If "television eats books," as novelist Larry Woiwode once wrote, *Sesame Street* is the Cookie Monster.

Sesame Street began with the loftiest of intentions. In 1967, Joan Ganz Cooney, a television producer hired by the Carnegie Corporation, developed an idea for a show "to promote the intellectual and cultural growth of preschoolers, particularly disadvantaged preschoolers." Educational television was nothing new, but it was known for its drabness; with immobile cameras frozen in front of droning professional types, it seemed an anachronism—the medium's "old maid," one wit called it. Cooney had the revolutionary idea of teaching through the jazzy techniques of commercial television: quick cuts, animation, humor.

In fact the model for the show was not so much the typical television program as the television ad. "We knew that young children watched a great deal of television in the years before they went to school," Cooney wrote later. "We knew also that they liked cartoons, game shows, situation comedies, . . . and above all, they were attracted by fast-paced, highly visual, oft-repeated commercials." Since kids like commercials, went the logic, give them commercials; only in this case "sell" them letters and numbers. Each hour would be "brought to you by" the letter H, say, or the number 9 instead of Sugar Pops or Frosted Flakes. It seemed brilliant in its obviousness.

But *Sesame Street*'s relationship to commercial television didn't stop there; in truth the show was devoured by the medium it set out to transform. Its enthrallment to the world of television and stardom is as fervid as that of the fans on Oscar night. Its shows are an encyclopedia of TV forms: minute-long soap operas with sappy organ music to teach the importance of trees, imitation MTV videos with a punk Muppet hostess to teach the letter N, game shows and their smarmy hosts, sitcoms, talk shows, TV award ceremonies—you name it. The Muppets spoof *Star Trek*, *The Twilight Zone*, *Jaws*, *The Addams Family*. Their musical numbers imitate Madonna, Cyndi Lauper, the Four Tops, the Beach Boys. On the rare occasions when superstars like Placido Domingo or Itzhak Perlman make guest appearances, kids might receive a sound bite of classical music. But any week's worth of viewing will ensure a comprehensive education in the history of rock and roll, from Elvis to Motown, from disco to rap. As I watched some Muppets imitating a rock-country group in long beards and trucker hats sing about the letter Z, my teenage daughter walked past and stared for a moment. "Hmm," she said, impressed. "ZZ Top."

From its inception, the Street has been a favorite destination for pop-culture celebrities: Johnny Cash, Jamie Lee Curtis, Gloria Estefan, Paul Simon, Meryl Streep, Lily Tomlin, Robin Williams, and dozens of other luminaries have all made appearances. Parents and older siblings, the show's creators reasoned, would be more likely to watch along with the house preschooler if they could catch a glimpse of a favorite movie star.

But however well-intentioned, by worshiping at television's glowing altar *Sesame Street* effectively ensures the conversion of the next generation to TV's beliefs and gods. When feminist groups denounced the all-male club of Bert, Ernie, Oscar, Elmo, and crew, the producers agreed to introduce Zoe, a girl who is "strong and has her own idea about things," in order to integrate the entrenched Muppet patriarchy. An unnecessary gesture: the show has girl role models aplenty—most of them devoted to demonstrating that C stands for celebrity. During one recent hour, a Madonna Muppet sang achingly of being a girl living "in a cereal world" now that she has agreed to eat cereal, a Bette Midler Muppet belted out the wonders of the divine M, and Ethel Mermaid outdid them both with a celebration of fish. The *Sesame Street* gal may have her own ideas about some things, but like most Americans she wants to be a star.

The tone that suffuses these sequences—humor spiced with irony—is only a very distant cousin of the slapstick that the show's research indicated children enjoyed. Instead, that tone is the junior version of TV's prevailing *Saturday Night Live* scoffing mode. In one "Monsterpiece Theater" segment, for instance, Alistair Cookie (a.k.a. the Cookie Monster) introduces this week's "exciting tale of international intrigue and suspense starring the famous spy and extremely cool guy, James Bond," in "Doctor No." The James Bond Muppet seeks out a specialist, Doctor No, for a problem no one else seems able to cure: he can't read the word "no."

The sequence displays an exquisite attentiveness to each hilarious detail: James Bond, with luxuriant black hair, sleuths in sunglasses and a raincoat; behind Doctor No is an eye chart with the word "no" in letters of decreasing size; Alistair Cookie sports a silk ascot and a velvet jacket and sits on a wing chair surrounded by leather-bound books and silver-framed pictures of fellow Muppets. The humor may not mean much to the thumb-sucking viewers more familiar with Jack Sprat than with James Bond, but sequences like these have their expensive impact and reinforce the easy fascination with the surfaces and rhythms of popular media. "Me love culture," Alistair Cookie mumbles through a mouthful of chocolate chips at the end of "Doctor No." Indeed.

This unwavering devotion to the tone and idiom of television powerfully homogenizes *Sesame Street*'s celebrated diversity. Sure, the rainbow cast is inclusive, embracing a deaf woman using sign language and a child in a wheelchair. Yet the show couldn't be more monocultural and conformist in its unwavering endorsement of American anti-intellectualism and cult of the cool. This attitude is dramatized on a subliminal level in the person of the pointy-headed Bert, the only creature to bring an air of vague maladjustment to this manically upbeat show. With his stiff, robotic laugh and his paper-clip collection, Bert is the cautionary if lovable Muppet-nerd counterpart to his cool, imaginative friend Ernie.

Most of the time, however, the message of hipness is less subtle. It's not just James Bond who is "an extremely cool

guy." Almost every hour contains some song explicitly flatter-
ing an idea of childhood beloved by Americans, one that
suffuses commercial TV and movies and especially advertisements: the child as energetic, sophisticated hipster. "I go to
school, school, school," rasps one Muppet rocker, shaking
his shaggy locks; "I'm so cool, cool, cool." This seems a
strange way to interest a young child in school; after all, part
of the charm of three-year-olds, at least those lacking a
Sesame Street education, is that they don't know the first
thing about cool.

Sometimes *Sesame Street* even falls into the familiar television subtext that TV is fun and exciting, while the life of
the mind is boring and stuffy. Teachers, professors, and scientists in cartoon segments invariably speak in dreary, pre-
tentious accents, often putting their audiences to sleep like
Annie Eyeball, Ph.D., who lectures stiffly on the virtues of
breathing. What's striking is how entirely gratuitous these
jabs are. To take only one example, in a recent nanosecond
segment, a child stands in front of his class to tell about a
case of hives. Look carefully and you'll see two of his classmates snoring at their desks—a remarkable message indeed
for preschool kids from the people bringing you your letters
and numbers.

If these criticisms sound a little crabby—after all, who
can resist the clever witticisms of sophisticated television?—
consider that the pleasures of *Sesame Street* purportedly
have never been for their own sake. The antics were only bait
to catch unsuspecting viewers for the show's higher purpose:
education. During the show's development, a group of eminent child experts formulated a curriculum according to
the latest academic theories about children's cognition. They
came up with a list of skills collected under categories
like "symbolic representation" (letters, numbers, geometric

shapes), "relational concepts" (up and down, near and far), and "perceptual discriminations" (identifying body parts).

Evidently the creators sensed that this skills-oriented vision of preschool education would not go over easily, for they simultaneously put another group of experts to work figuring out how to keep kids' eyes on the screen while they took their educational medicine. By using a "distracter" test—a slide show placed next to the television to determine at what moments fidgety viewers turned away from the TV screen—they discovered the power of visual pyrotechnics like fast-paced action, frequent cuts, and "pixilation" (a series of individual frames without connectors, so that characters move jerkily).

From the beginning, the show's creators were more entranced with their jazzy medium than with their message. And no wonder: they started out with the wrong message. The *Sesame Street* curriculum focuses on mere technical skills, the tools of mental cultivation rather than mental cultivation itself, the building blocks of thought rather than thought. Why anyone would want to read, what wider world literacy might unlock—on these questions of the purpose and value of the skills it teaches, *Sesame Street* is silent. Worse, the show's anti-intellectualism and its glorification of television culture over print send the implicit message that the skills of literacy have no meaningful purpose.

The show's technocratic educational curriculum, in other words, is inert and inconsequential. Stripped of all the noise and color, the fun and the speed, the sophisticated design-school aesthetic and the unfailing wittiness, it is nothing more than a disjointed series of animated flash cards (about forty per one-hour show), whose inherent blandness and triviality the producers spend millions trying to disguise. In one small fraction of one show, the three-year-old might be treated to a thirty-second flash of the letter T, a thirty-second rap on littering, a thirty-second Chinese design of the numbers 1 through 8, a one-minute skit by Muppets on the number 8, a two-minute song on cooperation, a thirty-second film clip of kids cooperating during a game, a one-minute rock-song animation of squares and triangles. Although the subject list has changed a bit over the years to include things like recycling and the increasingly fine points of self-esteem, the show's basic formula—breathing life into a bloodless curriculum through television glitz—has remained untouchable.

How bloodless? Take just one eloquent example: a Muppet holds up a picture of the Coliseum and pronounces it "a very old building that lots of people visit." Then she goes on to another tenuously related picture—completely missing the opportunity to kindle children's unfailing fascination with gladiators, perhaps even to tell the story of Androcles and the lion, and bring history to life.

But by now it should be clear that the creators of *Sesame Street* don't think much of children's curiosity. They inevitably strip the interest out of sequences concerned with subjects like animals or how things are made. The contrast between one *Sesame Street* segment and another on the same subject by the hopelessly square *Mister Rogers* captures the extent to which *Sesame Street* relies on seductive distracters instead of finding the interest in inherently interesting subjects. Guy Smiley, the frenzied Muppet game-show host, introduces a sneaker for a "This Is Your Life!" episode. With wild audience cheers in the background, the sneaker sighs and weeps as he is shown his birth in the mind of a designer, his first owner, and his old age in an abstract sculpture. Mister Rogers, on the other hand, shows a quiet seven-minute film of a sneaker factory, describing the actual production process from the stamping out of the rubber soles, to the molding of the canvas, to the boxing of the final product. For the next few minutes he talks about what the children have just seen. Without missing a beat, by contrast, the empty *Sesame Street* trifle dissolves into a glitzy thirty-second "ad" for the letter G.

According to the show's enthusiasts, this jumble is all very educational. Children learn to recognize letters and numbers as well as concepts like heavy and light ("You know you're heavy, baby, and I'm light," rasps a macho rock star in one segment), and in this way, enthusiasts argue, the show promotes the child's "emerging literacy." But there are several reasons to greet these claims with only one hand clapping. As any kindergarten teacher can tell you, identifying the letter A is about as central to reading as defining shortstop is to playing baseball—necessary but wildly insufficient. The skills required for reading are a complex mix of concentration, persistence, the linking of concepts, the mental recall of autonomous memories and images—the same skills that allow an older child to engage in analytic thinking. *Sesame Street*, by contrast, appeals to the most primal parts of the brain—its reflexive attraction to movement, light, and noise.

Still, as the sneaker episode demonstrates, the problem with *Sesame Street*'s approach to teaching children goes even deeper. For all the imaginativeness of its frenetic rhythms and dazzling surfaces, the show's triviality—indeed, the unrelenting trivialization of its pop-culture cool—does nothing to cultivate the deeper springs of children's imagination. What better way to develop children's emerging literacy and, one might add, hold their attention, than through stories of imaginative depth? As the psychoanalyst Bruno Bettelheim cautioned, "The idea that learning to read may enable one later to enrich one's life is experienced as an empty promise when the stories the child listens to, or is reading at the moment, are vacuous." On *Sesame Street*, vacuity is at the heart of every tale.

To be sure, researchers found early on in the show's planning that children were not likely to sit still for an adult reading, say, "Rapunzel" on the small screen. But they most certainly will sit still through dramatized or illustrated legends, fairy tales, and fables, as in a *Barney* segment, in which a girl of about nine read a story about an Eskimo child as the camera paused on each of the book's magnificent illustrations. After she finished, she took a minute to recall three of the more unfamiliar words in the story. The sequence offered an obvious way to expand a child's vocabulary, discipline his memory, nourish his sense of beauty, and enlarge his imagination.

This approach—or a puppet show or a Disney-style animation—could be used to retell traditional fairy tales and legends, from "Little Red Riding Hood" to "John Henry" to Odysseus. These stories have always stirred children's imaginations with their wolves, giants, heroes, and storms at sea. They also help the child master primal emotions, as Bettelheim memorably argued, while nurturing higher-order virtues like bravery, compassion, and loyalty. A child of three or four, after all, is not just a pleasure-obsessed skill machine; he is a puzzled newcomer looking for meaning and order in a world he barely knows.

Such a search is rendered meaningless on *Sesame Street*. Take its version of "Cinderella." A story that dramatizes the sense of unappreciated isolation that is inevitably a part of even the most loved child's experience, a parable that punishes envy and rewards hope, cools into shallow parody. Kermit the Frog in the belted mackintosh and brimmed hat sported by reporters in 1940s movies interviews Cinderella's prince, a dandy primping in his midnight-blue suit and admiring a glass slipper. Is he looking for the girl who stole his heart? No, he whines; he simply *must* own the other shoe.

A more telling example concerns Aesop's fable "The Tortoise and the Hare." In the original the tortoise's victory over the cocky hare demonstrates the virtues of persistence and modesty. A recent version of the fable by Caroline Castle, recommended by the authors of *Books That Build Character*, shows that the tale can be modernized and still maintain meaning. This version portrays the tortoise as "a retiring scholar living in a book-lined room and writing a huge tome . . . at the rate of two pages a day" and the hare as a narcissistic "fitness freak."

But look how *Sesame Street* travesties the same material. A girl Muppet named Prairie watches a buffoonish reenactment of the fable, in which the winner receives a new washer and dryer, and the tortoise is a smart-mouthed grandma ("Look out, baby, this is a Harley shell!"). Even souped up, the story is still too square for a girl of Prairie's sophistication; "I know, I know," she mocks in eye-rolling exasperation; "Slow and steady win the race." The segment ends with the hare turning on Prairie, who accidentally got in her way and caused her to lose; "You owe me a washer, girlie!" As in "Cinderella," the story is entirely drained of its meaning, and the hero is turned into a vain comic spouting one-liners; indeed, this spoof turns meaning itself into a joke.

Given all this glibness, it might seem encouraging to hear that this past season the producers began a "Let's Read and Write Campaign" after consulting with child experts about "what's new, what's important" in the field of early childhood education—perhaps implicitly acknowledging their failure on these grounds hitherto. Alas, the campaign only underscores the producers' dedication to television's flip style over a resonant substance. How do they go about teaching children that recent scientific discovery, "the wonder of books"? Why, according to the Children's Television Workshop's promotional literature, by bringing on celebrities like Lily Tomlin and the rap group Arrested Development, by parodies of books like "Donna Quixote," and by MTV-style videos, like the one in which the Muppet group "the Alphabeats" rock and roll in the library. In this way the *Sesame Street* tot is educated not in literacy but in television—its grammar, its rhythms, its stars, and, most subtly of all, its cool posture of the contemporary ironist too superior for curiosity, enchantment, or ideals. While this stance has become popular for school-age children in TV shows like *The Simpsons*, it is *Sesame Street*'s proud legacy to introduce it to kids still clutching their blankies and teddy bears.

The story of how Americans came to endow a show so completely wedded to the culture of television with deep educational significance is not an especially uplifting one. For the triumph of *Sesame Street* has less to do with quality than with a combination of savvy timing, sophisticated image-making, and vigorous promotion.

Sesame Street was born in the heated political atmosphere of the 1960s. Urban riots and early civil rights legislation had kindled a feeling of urgency about poor children's lagging school achievement. These concerns coalesced with child experts' growing belief that the cognitive abilities of all young children had been underestimated and underserved. Whereas early childhood had been considered a dreamy period of mommy-love, play, and wonder—what one expert called "the magic years"—and the phrase "early childhood education" had been almost unknown, now experts in cognitive development declared children avid, capable learners. In fact, stated Benjamin Bloom in *Stability and Change in Human Characteristics*, half of all learning was actually completed by age four.

Grammar school was too late to start repairing the deficits of childhood disadvantage. Early childhood programs aimed at the poor—Head Start, most notably—suddenly seemed the best route to improving inner-city children's academic chances and breaking the cycle of poverty. Although designed to appeal to all children, *Sesame Street* was also envisioned as an anti-poverty television program.

Sesame Street's time had come for two other reasons. First, American mothers, about to begin their double shift in the kitchen and at the office, would hardly be able to resist the most mesmerizing baby-sitter since Mary Poppins. And second, since preschool kids were already watching TV an average of thirty hours a week, why not turn that habit to advantage? The miserable state of commercial television had become a commonplace—a "vast wasteland," as FCC chairman Newton Minow famously put it in 1961. But even though, from *The Three Stooges* to *Flipper*, the pickings were slim, there were intriguing reports of children learning to read from observing letters on commercials, quiz shows, and weather reports.

Alert to all of these trends was Joan Ganz Cooney, the woman whom Carnegie Corporation president Lloyd Morrisett had hired to explore the potential of television for teaching children. Well connected and, in the words of former NET chairman John White, charming enough "to sell tea to the Chinese," Cooney had produced a documentary about a Harlem preschool and had won an Emmy for another educational television effort, "Poverty, Anti-Poverty, and the Poor." And her impressive credentials went beyond public television: she had also done a stint as a publicist at NBC.

Cooney brought to *Sesame Street* her shrewd grasp of the lessons of this still young and developing medium—its techniques both of production and of marketing. It was her idea not only to marry the two genres of commercial and educational television but also to bring that combination of glamour and sentiment that is the trademark of American show business to a lowly kids' show. She was intent on involving celebrities in *Sesame Street*. She molded the show's up-to-date aesthetic, which instantly made older educational models like *Romper Room* seem dowdy hand-me-downs. She shrewdly hired Jim Henson, whose Muppets—which had successfully advertised La Choy Chow Mein and Ivory Snow, among other products—remain *Sesame Street's* prime marketing symbol.

Knowing the importance of appealing to parents' pride in little Johnny's precocity, she supervised the transformation of the show from the arts-and-crafts projects and singing and clapping games outline in her original feasibility study to the jazzed-up letter-and-number flash cards. According to Gerald Lesser in *Children and Television: Lessons from Sesame Street*, this approach assured that kids could "feel good about knowing" something and gain "an important displayable skill" that parents could feel good about too.

With her publicist's eye, Cooney also intuited the advantage of a sentimental aura of un-self-interested benevolence for the whole project. Early on in the show's planning, she and Morrisett had unsuccessfully sought support from commercial networks. Rejection turned out to be a godsend. The show became, thanks to their marketing skill, Educational Television for the Good of Children, Particularly Poor Children, and the ironies of its love relationship with the television ad could be ignored. If this was entertainment, it was entertainment with an exalted mission, uncontaminated—or so it seemed—by profit motives and ratings lust.

In this and other ways, *Sesame Street* developed an image irresistible to the baby-boomer parents whose children were to form much of the show's audience. The host of the other educational offerings at the time, Mister Rogers, cardigan-clad and as square as a small-town minister, reminded them of dowdy Middle America, of their own Eisenhower child-hoods. But *Sesame Street? Sesame Street* was hip, urban—the creators believed they were taking a risk when they decided on a city street instead of the familiar picket-fence back-drop—and enlightened, as evidenced by its multiracial cast and its noncommercial broadcast home. The high-minded, public-service image in turn provided the show with a Teflon coating to which no criticisms—though they have trickled in steadily over the years—could stick.

From the outset the show was a hit, thanks in part to a promotional blitz orchestrated by the Carl Byoir agency and acknowledged by *Sesame Street* staffers to be "as extensive as had ever been attempted for any television project." In the first season alone, up to 36 percent of all children became regular viewers. Within two years Children's Television Workshop, originally a subsidiary of NET, became a separate nonprofit corporation. The workshop now boasts an income from product licensing, international television, and publish-ing of almost $120 million a year, an operations reserve fund of $34 million, and an endowment of $71 million. (*Sesame Street* costs about $20 million to produce annually.) CTW re-cently sold the rights for *Sesame Street*–related video- and audiotapes to Sony for an undisclosed amount and report-edly is looking for backers for a cable channel.

Many argue that *Sesame Street*'s success is a tribute to its scientifically proven educational benefits rather than image-making and publicity. But the CTW promotional machine has also effectively managed the vast amount of research on the show—a 1990 bibliography boasts more than a thousand entries. While negative studies gather dust in academic journals, their positive counterparts, often commissioned by the workshop, are faxed to a sympathetic, deadline-harried press and duly, sometimes literally, repeated. Yet many of those positive studies leave one with the feeling that experts ought to be spending more time with children actually watching the show. One especially egregious example claims the show offers a good means of encouraging vocabulary development because "the dialogue on *Sesame Street* closely resembles that of a mother talking to her child." Like what? "You know you're heavy, baby, and I'm light"?

Given closer scrutiny, two of the studies that CTW most frequently touts similarly hint at advocacy masquerading as social science. The Educational Testing Service (ETS), hired by the workshop early on and present at some initial planning sessions, supposedly demonstrated significant gains among viewers in a number of basic skills such as counting and naming letters and numbers. But a later Russell Sage Foundation review of the ETS data, under the direction of Northwestern University psychologist Thomas Cook, threw cold water on these results. Cook and his colleagues found very modest effects from the show, and even these gains they attributed to "encouragement to view"—the phone calls, promotional material, and weekly visits from ETS researchers to ensure an experimental group of regular viewers. Furthermore, they argued, whatever small value the show did have actually *increased* the intellectual gap between middle-class and poor children, exactly the opposite of the ETS findings.

More recent research, published by Aletha C. Huston and

On *Sesame Street*, It's All Show

John C. Wright of the Center for Research on the Influences of Television on Children, hardly even attempts to disguise its bias. Although they had not completed "in-depth analyses" of their data, the authors write, "there were practical, sentimental, academic, political, and personal reasons to complete the first report" of their findings in time for *Sesame Street*'s twenty-fifth anniversary. In fact, Huston and Wright, longtime advocates of educational television for children and previous CTW consultants, are "pleased" that their preliminary report can make the greatest claims yet for the show. Unlike most positive findings so far, which have merely asserted a correlation between watching *Sesame Street* and emerging literacy, Huston and Wright went so far as to state that watching the show "appears to play a positive causal role in [children's] development of readiness for school."

But if it's the show that causes school readiness, how does one explain that kids who watch *Sesame Street* frequently also spend more time looking at books, at "art, music, paper and pencil games, . . . cultural events," as Huston and Wright also note? Somebody who cares about the children's future is taking them to the circus, buying them art supplies, and turning PBS on at the appropriate time—and it's not Big Bird. Oddly, in a 1991 article, one not commissioned by CTW, these same authors seem to have understood that kids who watch educational TV come from different sorts of homes than kids watching commercial television; they "have parents who also provide them with stimulating toys and activities, and who are attentive and affectionate to them. Children who frequently watch cartoons and other pure entertainment programs come from homes with lower levels of stimulation and affection."

The sum total of the positive studies of *Sesame Street* ends up a puzzlement. To show *Sesame Street*'s broad reach, CTW touts a Westat survey suggesting that 77 percent of all American preschoolers, including 87 percent of black children and 79 percent of Hispanic, watch the show once a week or more. To prove its educational benefits, the workshop hypes other studies that purportedly show its viewers to be more cooperative, more school-ready, and more likely to demonstrate signs of emerging literacy. But if 77 percent of American children are regularly watching a show so miraculously beneficial, why do kindergarten teachers, according to *Ready to Learn*, a report put out by the Carnegie Foundation for the Advancement of Teaching in 1991, find their students increasingly deficient in language skills?

Though CTW is now embarking on a study to prove *Sesame Street*'s impact as late as high school, the truth is obvious to anyone who can forget about statistical correlations and control groups for a minute: no single television show will ever turn children into literate students. Yet the myth that *Sesame Street* does just that has helped propel CTW into not just critical but commercial success.

And what a rich irony that is: the very image of *Sesame Street* as a noncommercial educational alternative to the flimflam of advertisers and network television has helped CTW make a fortune selling merchandise to children. "A for-profit company would have killed the golden goose," Cooney told *Working Woman* magazine in 1986. CTW has licensed more than five thousand products, including close to four hundred in 1994 alone: *Sesame Street* books, bubble bath, clocks, lunch boxes, tapes, toys, videos, Chef Boy-Ar-Dee *Sesame Street* pasta ("formulated to meet the nutritional needs of preschoolers"), and the *Sesame Street* Silly Sentence Maker ("helps kids say really goofy things but in a grammatically correct fashion").

Kids can shop in *Sesame Street* General Stores, where

they can buy an "oustanding array of quality products that demonstrate and are compatible with *Sesame Street*'s teaching goals"—items like the "Streetwise" line of underwear and jammies, sheets and blankets, necklaces, bracelets, and earrings.

This commercialization might seem inconsequential if the show truly were "quality programming" in the public interest. It is not. While it teaches the alphabet and supposedly prepares children for school, it actually instructs them in the conventions of an anti-intellectual pop culture and thus makes common cause with the vast contemporary forces arrayed against literacy. While it asserts its purity from commercial taint, it wields the most sophisticated marketing strategies to sell its products to keep the show in business. Like the television commercial on which it is modeled, *Sesame Street* is a triumph of appearance over substance.

[1995]

4

Raising Children for an Uncivil Society

Recently I rebuked my nine-year-old daughter for some especially obnoxious back talk. "It's a free country," she retorted with that know-it-all sneer second nature to her generation. Her words, familiar ammunition in living-room wars for decades now, point to one of the cultural contradictions of American childhood. In order to become individuals capable of self-determination—capable of freedom—we need years of surveillance, orders, and control. It's a free country, maybe, but it takes a heavily regulated living room.

For it's in the living room that children undergo what sociologist Norbert Elias calls the "civilizing process." During their early years children must be taught to make a habit of the self-restraint required for life in society, to control and modify their raw impulses and drives. Many Americans, secure in their own successful completion of this process, have come to take basic moral education for granted or to assume our liberated age can go easy on it. But in a free, temptation-filled society, the civilizing process needs to be more demanding than ever; individuals who will grow up to live in coed dorms or military barracks, for instance, must develop a massive and reliable system of inner controls. In truth, every society must be able to inculcate the young with dependable controls. "Every scheme of ethics demands that in important respects we practice self-restraint," the political theorist Clifford Orwin has written. "We all first come to know morality, and for the most part continue to know it, as denial." Or as the sociologist Phillip Rieff puts it, "The moral life begins with renunciation."

Every culture goes about the civilizing process in its own way in order to shape citizens fitted to its requirements: as Plato understood, child-rearing is a form of politics. In the early days of the republic, Americans overthrew the harsh Calvinist discipline founded on fear and absolute obedience to introduce a new child-rearing that appealed to children's affections and emerging reason. Instead of breaking a child's will, Americans began gently shaping his personality. They recognized, as did foreign visitors who commented on this new democratic American family, that the young democracy required a new man, independent and self-governing.

What they didn't recognize was how laden their new mode of child-rearing was with paradox and contradiction. Parents had simultaneously to teach the habits of restraint and freedom. They had to suppress the child's egotism while cultivating his personal ambition, to instill respect for authority while nurturing critical independence, to teach convention while celebrating ingenuity, to encourage a loving commitment toward family and tradition while promoting flexibility and autonomy. If juggling the conflicting demands of autonomy and self-control seemed a difficult acrobatic performance, it nevertheless worked. Americans *were* different: flexible, creative, entrepreneurial, improvisational, but held in check by the invisible cords of cultural prohibitions.

Today, though, to read the recommendations of mainstream American child experts is to conclude that this delicate balance has collapsed. Our era's equation is all autonomy, with no restraint. As James Q. Wilson has observed, in a number of recent works on moral development the subject of self-control is entirely absent. And why should it be otherwise? The experts' child is free of dark urges. His heart is full of compassion, his head packed with moral wisdom. Adults do not need to shape him; he is so clearheaded and sensible as to be capable almost of raising himself. In fact, adult efforts at "civilizin'," as Huck Finn called it, endanger this child, distorting his unique personality and his fundamental goodness. That's the myth, at any rate: call it the American Child Pastoral. The reality, with today's soaring rates of child crime, depression, and disaffection, suggests that the current crop of child-rearing experts have got it wrong.

They go wrong by unwittingly proving the rule well known to politicians and other malefactors: half-truths can be as misleading as outright lies. Dr. Benjamin Spock, whose *Baby and Child Care* has sold at rates second only to the Bible, is a prime case in point. He begins by defining children as social creatures, an observation few would dispute. But this clear truth dissolves into an Enlightenment fairy tale; the child Spock describes is also sensible, moderate, self-regulating, and rational, the opposite of the mysteriously primitive, anarchic, sleep-destroying creature most parents know and love. "Your baby is born to be a reasonable, friendly human being," he begins, unexceptionably enough. "Most babies have a natural tendency to establish a regular pattern of feeding and sleeping," he continues, more fancifully; they "just naturally tend . . . to fit into the family's schedule." You would never know from Spock that most babies naturally do to a family's schedule, not to mention its house, what Caligula did to Rome. Nor would you learn that rationality and regular habits do not occur spontaneously but come about largely through the energetic, day-in, day-out efforts of parents.

No, by nature Spock's child is more temperate than any philosopher. When it comes to weaning, the doctor suggests, "Take it easy and follow your baby's lead"; most babies, he says, willingly give up their pacifiers by three or four months—a fact my neighbor would be surprised to hear, having just gone cold turkey with her two-year-old, an experience that reminded her of her worst days as a volunteer at a drug rehab center. Feeding? No problem. Go ahead and feed her if you think she is hungry, he advises: "If you are mistaken, she'll merely refuse to take much."

Faith in children's natural good judgment appears in the most unlikely times and places. During toilet training, for instance: "The most that parents can do is guide them a little," Spock assures readers. "If a mother will realize that the baby will mostly 'train' himself," he writes, endorsing the methods of another famed pediatrician and author of top-selling advice books, T. Berry Brazelton, "children should become trained of their own free will—no coercion at all." Another popular work, *What to Expect: The Toddler Years*, responds to the question, "When is it time to begin?" with what has become conventional wisdom: "Look no further than your toddler for the answer. Only your child can tell you."

The experts can't ignore those occasions when children exhibit behavior that might seem a little, well . . . contrary. But don't be fooled; this is not what it seems, writes Penelope Leach, a British psychologist with a huge following in the United States—*Your Baby and Child* alone has sold well over a million and a half copies. Leach allows that a two-year-old might "rush around the room, wild and screaming, . . . fling himself on the floor, writhing, kicking, and screaming as if he were fighting with demons. He may scream and scream until he makes himself sick. He may scream and turn blue in the face."

This Neanderthal display might turn parents pale in the face, but to Leach this is a wrong response. They should be *proud*. "Your toddler is rapidly developing a sense of being a separate, independent person with personal rights, preferences, and ploys," she writes. "His 'willfulness' is a sign that he is growing up and that he feels secure enough at present to try to manage things for himself." "Open negativism toward his parents is a toddler's way of expressing his need for independence," Brazelton writes in *Toddlers and Parents* in nearly identical words. "With his 'no' he establishes himself as separate from his parents. Every time he says 'no' or acts out a negative response to a demand from those around him, he is learning about himself as a separate individual."

This spin on the temper tantrum transmutes the young child—still only at the early stages of the civilizing process, when raw impulses are under only intermittent control—into a pint-size Minuteman, just looking after his independence and rights. This is an incomparable act of revisionism; the little dictator has been mythologized into a heroic revolutionary, the Declaration of Independence in hand.

True, no one suggests indulging the tantrum. Experts judiciously recommend a wait-out-the-storm response, nicely balancing the tension between suppressing the child's egotism and accepting his self-assertion. But a dangerous note of admiration creeps in. "Toddlers who have a lot of tantrums," Leach assures us, "are usually lively children who may be highly intelligent. They know what they want to do; they want to do a great many things, and they mind a great deal when someone or something prevents them."

From a less-known but similarly optimistic work, *The*

Emotional Life of the Toddler, parents learn that the tantrum is a "wonderfully eloquent if seldom appreciated expression of the toddler's inner experience," whose underlying theme is, "No, I am not your clone, and I will not relinquish my sense of myself to do what you want me to do and be who you want me to be." Who could resist admiring the clear-eyed self-confidence of such a rebel?

Ignoring the reality of the temper tantrum in this fashion does not reflect an isolated lapse in psychological judgment. The truth is, much as you might read about antisocial behavior in the newspaper, it seldom makes an appearance in the literature of child psychology. The experts are in denial. Yes, they occasionally give us a glimpse of aggression or envy, but these do not appear as the stubborn urges that throughout human history have necessitated moral codes and laws (not to mention police). Rather, they are "stages," that is, passing moods to be passively endured instead of actively tamed. The historian Peter Stearns nicely captures this evasion when he points out that while Victorian and early-twentieth-century child-rearing books addressed children's cruelty toward animals, more recent manuals tend to fret over their fear *of* them.

If not aggression and appetite, what impulses *are* part of the child's natural endowment, according to modern experts? Their most usual answer: empathy. The naturalness of empathy, an old philosophical notion popularized by the eighteenth-century earl of Shaftesbury, is an idea worth taking seriously. Academic experts, in particular, correctly point to the many examples of what appears to be the spontaneous empathy of children familiar to parents: the eighteen-month-old who brings his mother to comfort a crying playmate, the three-year-old whose eyes fill with tears at the sight of an injured dog. But our pastoralists turn a grain of truth into a universe of wishful thinking. They go much further than concluding that human beings are naturally empathic in the way that they are, say, naturally fearful or naturally curious. They see empathy as the principal engine of moral life. This overestimation is no mere academic error. For by overstating the naturalness and power of empathy, they shift the foundation of morality away from self-control and toward self-expression.

According to a central strand of current thinking, empathy is such a basic human instinct that it makes its first appearance in the hospital nursery along with the sucking and startle reflexes. When newborns fuss at the sound of another baby's cry, according to William Damon, a professor at Brown University and author of *The Moral Child: Nurturing Children's Natural Moral Growth*, they are demonstrating the "spontaneous tendency to identify with another's discomfort. . . . Here we see, in the primitive world of the crib, one human sharing another's burdens." For the older child, empathy is automatic or "largely involuntary if one pays attention to the victim," according to Martin Hoffman, a professor at New York University and one of the foremost experts in the field of moral development. The parents' role is simply to draw the child's attention to the pain of others. When they do so, the child experiences guilt, which Hoffman calls "empathic distress." The older children grow, the more cognitive sophistication they can bring to their understanding of others' pain, and the less they need adults to point out others' suffering. According to Hoffman, this natural moral development explains the tendency of adolescents to identify with the plight of distant, oppressed peoples.

Questions leap to the mind of any parent. If empathy is so powerful, why do well-socialized children feel so little of it when it comes to the wailing sister whose doll they have just beheaded? And why are well-nurtured teenagers so lacking in this natural feeling when it comes to the suffering that their flagrant rudeness causes their parents? One would assume that we would extend empathy most readily to those we love, yet the truth known to all experienced in family life is often otherwise. Empathy theorists have nothing to say about psychic conflict, ambivalence, or the child's taste for cruelty (unless it is caused by profound neglect or abuse); they have rejected the universal model of morality as self-restraint. In their view, children do good because they have no strong desire to do anything else.

To their credit, empathy theorists have not shied away from talking about guilt, a subject many academic psychologists have shunned in recent decades. Indeed, the fact that today's experts give the impulse credit at all appears to mark an important cultural shift. For many decades psychologists have yearned to banish guilt as an exacting, soul-killing, almost Victorian imposition of duty and sexual repression. Though for Freud guilt was so central to good behavior that it had its own throne in the superego, from where it pronounced sentence over all thoughts and deeds, by mid-century psychologists began to attack this traditionally understood mechanism of self-restraint. It was a source of neurosis, they argued, of pleasure-denying inhibition and low self-confidence. Fear, self-contempt, anxiety: these were not emotions suitable to a newly affluent, pleasure-seeking age, and guilt fell into disrepute among the learned.

In order for guilt to be revived as a useful emotion, as is happening among some academics today, it had to undergo a stylish makeover from its prim past. Distinguished from both Freud's neurosis factory and the more generalized old-fashioned call of duty, it has been resurrected as, in Hoffman's words, "a true interpersonal guilt—the bad feeling one

has about oneself because one is aware of harming someone." In this benign retelling of its origins, guilt is drained of
hot, red-faced shame, and the guilty individual is transformed from the hero of a Greek tragedy to the heroine of a
sentimental novel. Now doing right requires no self-denial;
when we do good we are merely expressing ourselves.
Closely allied with sympathy and imagination, the child's
guilt (the result of projecting himself into the painful experience of another) confirms not his immoral longings but his
noble and fine nature.

Newborns whose screams offer proof of human compassion, toddlers whose tantrums are demands for self-
determination, schoolchildren whose guilty looks are
evidence of natural empathy: it is easy enough to criticize
the benign optimism of the American Child Pastoral. But
surveys suggest that American parents go along with at least
the general tenor of these ideas. According to researchers
Sigurdur Gretarsson and Donna Gelfand, they tend to see
friendliness and generosity as innate to their children's dis-
position; undesirable behavior like rudeness or irritability,
on the other hand, they view as "transitory and extrinsically
caused."

Worse, the myth of the American Child Pastoral hints to
parents that moral instruction can actually harm their children. For behind the myth lies a powerful set of assumptions
about personal identity shared by many Americans: each individual possesses a unique and worthy inner core, an essential "authentic" identity that must have ample opportunity to
express its being. This idea of an authentic self goes much
further than more traditional forms of individualism, which
celebrate self-determination of beliefs, opinions, and life
choices. It insists on a far more expansive freedom: I must be

allowed to speak out or act not because I must discover for myself what's true or right but because it expresses my feelings, the "real" me. Self-restraint—that is, the civilizing process itself—runs the risk of inhibiting, or "disrespecting," this authentic self.

This exaggerated respect for the authentic self places our experts in a bind when it comes to advice about how to teach manners. Children everywhere learn manners very early in their development, for manners offer the particular habitual forms of behavior that promote harmonious social life. But American experts are grudging, almost tongue-tied, on this subject. After all, manners often require individuals to restrain their personal inclinations; they are necessarily formulaic and often insincere—the very opposite of true expressions of feeling. Spock tries to bypass the problem this poses for the authentic self by proffering the following sunny advice: "Teaching children to say 'Please' or 'Thank you' is really not the first step. The most important thing is to have them like people." Note the good doctor's serious misdiagnosis. The purpose of saying please and thank you is not, in fact, to confirm our friendly feelings; it is to acknowledge the efforts others make on our behalf in a ritualized form, precisely so that we do not depend on the vagaries of feeling.

Spock completely recasts the goal of manners from reining in egotism to venting it. To him, far more important than how children behave is what they are. In a similar vein, the authors of *What to Expect: The Toddler Years* warn us, "Children who are nagged about their manners or are punished for not saying 'thank you' or for not using a fork . . . won't feel positive about manners and are likely to ignore them completely whenever they are out from under the eye of the enforcing parent." At any rate, not to worry. According to

Spock, "Good manners come naturally"—thus making the reader suspect that the world's premier pediatrician *never, ever spent a day with a child*.

So our experts transform parents from authorities who teach—sometimes sternly—the renunciations and manners that make social life possible into facilitators, cheerfully escorting the child's own unique self into maturity. At its most extreme, authenticity makes parental authority entirely unnecessary. "I never use the expression 'motivate a child,'" asserts one expert in a "Parent and Child" column in the *New York Times*. "All we can do is influence how they motivate themselves." In the same spirit, Penelope Leach writes, "There is no virtue in facing children with absolute 'dos' and 'don'ts,'" adding, with no comprehension of her illogic, "Rules are very useful in keeping a small child safe. But they really don't play much part in teaching him how to behave." Leach, who likes to put the word *discipline* in quotation marks, sees every parent as a potential martinet: "A gradual and gentle exposing of the child to the results of his own ill-advised actions is the only ultimate sanction you need. Any other kind of punishment is revenge and power-mongering." The authors of another aptly titled advice book, *Your Child Is Smarter Than You Think*, show a similar abhorrence of parental authority: "Simply telling your child not to do something—'Don't do that'—often said in an understandably exasperated tone of voice, is the least effective way of helping your child learn and understand self-control. It's an overt power play."

True, a suspicion of authority is central to the American outlook. And certainly many of our experts' suggestions—such as giving children reasons for rules or allowing small negotiations over them—when done in moderation with older children are fine means of promoting independent minds capable of carrying on that tradition. But what was once a healthy wariness about raw power has hardened into a debilitating taboo familiar to many middle-class American parents. Experts reveal it in the way they advise parents, particularly those with toddlers, to engage in almost any charade to hide the fact that they are in charge: bargaining, just-a-few-minutes-more negotiating, bribing. Leach tells parents of toddlers that they will need not only patience and good humor but "talent as an actor too. Are you in a hurry to get home? If you swoop the toddler into his stroller when he wanted to walk, all hell will break loose. Act as if you had all the time in the world, offer to be a horse and pull him home, and you will get there as fast as your legs will take the two of you." If your child refuses to get out of the stroller, counsel the authors of *What to Expect*, "Suggest, perhaps, that the dog get in the stroller or pretend to get in it yourself. . . . Give orders pretending you're a dog or a lion, Big Bird, Mickey Mouse." Anything but a parent.

A new crop of child-rearing books, supposedly more realistic about children's need for unambiguous guidance, does more to reveal the powerful hold of the American Child Pastoral than to offer a new vision. Robert Coles's best-selling *The Moral Intelligence of Children*, for instance, asserts that parents and teachers are not offering enough moral instruction. But this claim is at odds with his real conclusions, as revealed in his title: that children are naturally moral—no, better than that, "morally intelligent." Coles ponders children's observations as if they were the pearls of Zen masters. He evokes "the stillness of bodies, the rapt attention," and the children's "moral vitality" during his classroom discussions with them. A treasured anecdote, repeated in several interviews, demonstrates the wisdom of his injured nine-year-old son, who—imagine the empathy!—tells his dad to slow down while racing to the hospital because he might cause an accident. "My son had become my moral instructor," Coles marvels.

This ambivalence—between advocating a strong role for parents in shaping children and trusting overmuch in children's innate gifts—runs throughout American advice literature. On the one hand, experts dislike uncivil behavior and offer some useful advice about managing children. Coles and Brazelton, for instance, both counsel that responding to every infant demand runs the risk of turning them into tyrants. But by getting all misty about children's natural morality, independence, and authenticity, they undermine their point.

Their solution to this ambivalence is to reduce discipline to "setting limits." They ignore the important distinction between setting limits and defining moral norms. Parents setting limits are only placing boundaries on the child's self-expression. Parents defining moral norms—both negative norms of what you don't do and positive ones of what you should do—are teaching right and wrong. They are passing on a rich inheritance of principles and rituals that the child does not possess by nature and can only acquire from his culture, primarily through the teachings of his parents.

Experts have little advice to offer parents about this positive side of the task of raising children. They cannot imagine how adults induct children into the man-made world of morals and manners. In their mythology, our *wunderkinder* construct their own moral identity with a minimum of parental or social interference. Instead of developing a superego to represent society's interdictions in the mind, these kids need only empathy and its sister, guilt, both of them natural parts of the self. They do not need to learn the expectations of others and the forms for satisfying them;

they need to learn only themselves. And so, in the guise of science, experts unwittingly advance a radical individualism. Rather than a recipe for a democratic personality that delicately balances personal ambition and public obligation, they have concocted a formula for egotists inept at forming attachments or seeing themselves as part of a larger whole. This is precisely the sort of egotism that Tocqueville viewed as latent in American life, an egotism that "saps the virtues of public life" and that produces "people . . . far too much disposed to think exclusively of their own interests, to become self-seekers practicing a narrow individualism and caring nothing for the public good."

The best illustration of this failure of moral understanding can be found in the works of our two most important theorists of moral development, Lawrence Kohlberg and Carol Gilligan, whose distrust of moral authority—parental or otherwise—knows no bounds. Kohlberg, a professor of psychology at Harvard until his death in 1987 and a touchstone thinker for child developmentalists for over twenty years, believed that moral development progresses through six stages. In the lower stages, common to all children, moral reasoning is based on authority and convention. At the higher stages, the individual reasons not according to local and subjective concerns but by appealing to abstract principles. For instance, my daughter was at the lowly stage two when someone asked her at age five why she shouldn't take a piece of candy from the corner store, and she answered, "Because I might get into trouble." Unlike the older stage-five or -six adolescent, who can argue from more general principles of fairness, her naive mind could conceive of right and wrong only through their personification in authority.

Kohlberg's claim that good behavior is a result of mature reasoning never found much proof in the real world; one study of incarcerated juveniles, for instance, found that these malefactors could reason abstractly quite as well as a control group of their law-abiding peers. But his theory had the virtue of confirming several bedrock principles of the American Child Pastoral. For one thing, the Kohlbergian child does not appear to have any unruly impulses to control. Further, Kohlberg was not in the least interested in the way morality might reveal itself in particular forms of manners, rules of etiquette, or dos and don'ts. And last, adults have only a walk-on role in shaping children's moral life. As he wrote in the essay "The Young Child as Philosopher" (grandfather of *The Moral Child* and *The Moral Intelligence of Children*), "Children think for themselves. The basic ideas of children do not come directly from adults or other children and will be maintained in spite of adult teaching." Children learn to reason in accordance with a prewired biological schedule. The most we can do is nudge them into the next stage.

No one goes further than Kohlberg in rejecting traditional moral education. Believing that only mature reasoning would lead the individual to an acceptance of "justice, rights, and the Golden Rule," he derided any attempt to introduce children to particular goods, famously dubbing it the "bag of virtues" approach. The whole moral inheritance of social norms and religious codes has nothing to offer the growing child; to the contrary, they run the risk of stifling his moral autonomy. Asked by parents and teachers why so many of his recommended lessons seemed to lead to the conclusion that children should resist authority, he scoffed, "Such teachers do not believe moral behavior should be based on reasoning. Rather, it should be based on the adult's preaching and on stories and situations that affirm the child's faith in the adult's authority." Like the democratic toddler we saw earlier, the healthy individual is the one who does not submit readily to his parents or rules. To become moral, the child has only to retreat in solitary meditation to the private monastery of his mind.

But Kohlberg did not see how completely his own individualistic moral system, which culminated in what he considered nature's law, was in fact the product of inherited prejudices rather than abstract reasoning. As one anthropologist objected, Kohlberg believed ethical maturity would necessarily lead one to oppose "capital punishment, hierarchy, tribalism, and divine authority." We should have known: nature's highest moral achievement is a Harvard professor.

Kohlberg's student, Carol Gilligan, is commonly understood to have moderated her teacher's celebration of autonomy, but in reality she has taken his ideas about a naturally self-generated morality to a new extreme. Her revolutionary first book, *In a Different Voice*, was a milestone of feminist thought both inside and outside the academy, influencing everyone from ed-school faculty to management consultants. Gilligan argued that Kohlberg and other theorists of moral development had told the story only from a man's point of view, as an ascent toward greater personal autonomy and mastery of abstract rules of justice. From this vantage point, women, who tend to be more embedded in relationships and to look for meaning in concrete situations, inevitably appeared deviant or immature. Gilligan made a plea for a distinctive feminine moral sense, what she called an "ethic of care," to supplement the already deified male "ethic of justice."

Gilligan's fame intensified to stardom—in 1996 *Time* pronounced her one of the twenty-five most influential Americans—when in her later books she advanced a notion that has now become conventional wisdom: that girls, as they enter adolescence, suffer a loss of self-esteem. Her account of how this happens is a remarkable instance of the American Child Pastoral.

Gilligan's moral biography of girlhood reads like this: Until preadolescence a young girl's relationships, the central arena of her moral development, are guileless and open, or, as Gilligan says, "genuine." She knows what she wants from others and asks for it without fuss. Even her conflicts smell sweet. Once she has "judge[d] which disagreements are worth having," says Gilligan, she enters into them with clarity and good sense. Girls of this age, with their "rich emotional lives," are perfectly authentic creatures; they "speak of their thoughts and feelings about relationships in direct ways." This authenticity leads them to "wisdom and generosity" and, in the words of a colleague Gilligan quotes approvingly, "a profound sense of morality." These untainted beings are not just morally intelligent—they're geniuses.

But then shades of the prison house begin to close about the growing girl. They "approach the wall of shoulds"; they are forced to endure "psychological foot-binding" as their spirits are crushed by the exacting requirements of the world around them. They fall under "the tyranny of the nice and the kind," as Gilligan labels their moral education. " 'Nice' girls are always calm, controlled, quiet," she writes. "They never cause a ruckus; they are never noisy, bossy, or aggressive; they are not anxious; they do not cause trouble." Though the viciously cliquish Laurel School in Cleveland— where her 1992 book, *Meeting at the Crossroads* (written with Lyn Mikel Brown), was researched—often resembles an all-girl revue of *Lord of the Flies*, Gilligan is convinced that these girls have undergone not too little of the civilizing process but too much. By forbidding the easygoing, naturally occurring conflicts of girls' early years and thereby suppressing

their authenticity, she argues, adults poison their organic relationships. The once lively, honest girls lose their "voice"
and succumb to doubt, self-abnegation, and "silence."

Like her teacher, Gilligan goes to the limit in her dismissal of socializing authority. For her, what has universally
been recognized as the work of civilization—the growing
child's gains in self-control, her increasing civility—is
"tyranny." In *Meeting at the Crossroads*, an eleven-year-old recalls that when she was younger, "I had more fights or arguments." But now she has learned that "I'm not always right;
[my friends] could have been just as right, and they have
their thoughts too." Some might find this touching evidence
of nascent maturity, but not Gilligan. She frets that the girl
"has to suspend what she really feels . . . which, in effect, re-
moves her from genuine relationship." She makes a similar
judgment about Lauren, whose mother has encouraged her
to "think before she speaks or acts." Lauren tells how she
thinks back to her mother's advice and agrees to share the
computer with a classmate instead of fighting over it. Gilligan can only worry about "what Lauren gives up by playing
by these rules." At ten, Noura no longer wants "to fight over
the stupid little things" with her brother, Gilligan reports. According to this vulgar Wordsworth of the girls' school,
"Noura is beginning, it seems, to disconnect from her feelings and knowledge in an attempt to connect to what others
want."

It is the rebellious younger girls who "refuse to take no
for an answer" who earn Gilligan's respect. When Lauren,
who ponders resisting "a really dumb" school assignment,
gives in and does her homework, Gilligan haughtily registers
her disapproval. "No one," she remarks, "seems to notice
that Lauren doesn't say what she wants." On the other hand,
Karin, who stalks out of her class because her teacher fails to

call on her, gets credit for "blow[ing] the whistle on relational violations." "The capacity for these eight-year-olds to be openly angry—to be 'really mad'—to be disruptive and resistant," she enthuses, "gives them an air of unedited authority and authenticity." Girls who resist doing their homework, who argue with their teachers, who rebel against their mothers, who fight with their friends: this is moral health as envisioned by one of America's premier psychologists.

What's especially unsettling about all this is that Gilligan has been hailed as our great philosopher of interconnectedness, the corrector of our American (and putatively male) infatuation with autonomy. The truth is, Gilligan is even *more* radical than her peers when it comes to authentic individualism. She disdains the very idea of self-control and seeks to remove girls from this universally recognized requirement of civilization. And while she celebrates "relationships," she has no patience whatever with the demands for mutual accommodation and forbearance they inevitably make on us.

Gilligan's more general—and depressingly familiar—failure is that she cannot evoke for her readers the adult's role in introducing children to their basic obligations. Like her fellow child experts, she promotes the myth of an autonomous child-artist who can design his own moral picture. The danger, as we are discovering, is that the picture will be an ugly one. At the very least, the myth leads to nonsensical conclusions: that we can live in society but be completely self-made, that we can be attached but unencumbered, that we can have relationships without obligations.

No country can be that free.

[1997]

5

Who Killed School Discipline?

Ask Americans what worries them most about the public schools, and the answer might surprise you: discipline. For several decades now, poll after poll shows it topping the list of parents' concerns. Recent news stories—from the Columbine massacre, to Jesse Jackson's protests against the expulsion of six brawling Decatur, Illinois, high school students, to the killing of one Flint, Michigan, six-year-old by another—guarantee that the issue won't lose its urgency any time soon.

Though fortunately only a small percentage of schools will ever experience real violence, the public's sense that something has gone drastically wrong with school discipline isn't mistaken. Over the past thirty years or so, the courts and the federal government have hacked away at the power of educators to maintain a safe and civil school environment. Rigid school bureaucracies and psychobabble-spouting "experts" have twisted such authority as remains into alien—and alienating—shapes, so that kids today are more likely than ever to go to disorderly schools, whose only answers to the disorder are ham-fisted rules and therapeutic techniques designed to manipulate students' behavior, rather than to initiate them into a genuine civil and moral order. What's been lost is educators' crucial role of passing on cultural values to the young and instructing them in how to behave through innumerable small daily lessons and examples. If the children become disruptive and disengaged, who can be surprised?

School discipline today would be a tougher problem than ever, even without all these changes, because of the nationwide increase of troubled families and disorderly kids. Some schools, especially those in inner cities, even have students who are literally violent felons. High school principal Nora Rosensweig of Green Acres, Florida, estimates that she has had twenty to twenty-five such felons in her school in recent years, several of them sporting the electronic ankle bracelets that keep track of paroled criminals. "The impact that one of those students has on a hundred kids is amazing," Rosensweig observes. Some students, she says, find them frightening. Others, intrigued, see them as rebel heroes.

But today principals lack the tools they used to have for dealing with even the unruliest kids. Formerly they could expel such kids permanently or send them to special schools for the hard-to-discipline. The special schools have largely vanished, and state education laws usually don't allow for permanent expulsion. So at best a school might manage to transfer a student felon elsewhere in the same district. New York City principals sometimes engage in a black-humored game of exchanging these "Fulbright Scholars," as they jokingly call them: "I'll take two of yours if you take one of mine, and you'll owe me."

Educators today also find their hands tied when dealing with another disruptive—and much larger—group of pupils, those covered by the 1975 Individuals with Disabilities Education Act (IDEA). This law, which mandates that schools provide a "free and appropriate education" for children regardless of disability—and provide it, moreover, within regular classrooms whenever humanly possible—effectively strips educators of the authority to transfer or to suspend for long periods any student classified as needing special education.

This wouldn't matter if special education included mainly the wheelchair-bound or deaf students whom we ordinarily think of as disabled. But it doesn't. Over the past several decades, the number of children classified under the vaguely defined disability categories of "learning disability" and "emotional disturbance" has exploded. Many of these kids are those once just called "unmanageable" or "antisocial": part of the legal definition of emotional disturbance is "an inability to build or maintain satisfactory interpersonal relationships with peers and teachers"—in other words, to be part of an orderly community. Prosecutors will tell you that disproportionate numbers of the juvenile criminals they now see are special-ed students.

With IDEA restrictions hampering them, school officials can't respond forcefully when these kids get into fights, curse teachers, or even put students and staff at serious risk, as too often happens. One example captures the law's absurdity. School officials in Connecticut caught one student passing a gun to another on school premises. One, a regular student, received a yearlong suspension, as federal law requires. The other, disabled (he stuttered), received just a forty-five-day suspension and special individualized services, as IDEA requires. Most times, though, schools can't get even a forty-five-day respite from the chaos these kids can unleash. "They are free to do things in school that will land them in jail when they graduate," says Bruce Hunter, an official of the American Association of School Administrators. Laments Julie Lewis, staff attorney for the National School Boards Association: "We have examples of kids who have sexually assaulted their teacher and are then returned to the classroom."

Discipline in the schools isn't primarily about expelling sex offenders and kids who pack guns, of course. Most of the time, what's involved is the "get your feet off the table" or "don't whisper in class" kind of discipline that allows teachers to assume that kids will follow the commonplace directions they give hundreds of times daily. Thanks to two Supreme Court decisions of the late 1960s and the 1970s, though, this everyday authority has come under attack too.

The first decision, *Tinker v. Des Moines School District*, came about in 1969 after a principal suspended five high school students for wearing black armbands in protest against the Vietnam War. *Tinker* found that the school had violated students' free-speech rights. "It can hardly be argued," wrote Justice Abe Fortas for the majority, "that students or teachers shed their constitutional rights to free speech or expression at the schoolhouse gate." Schools cannot be "enclaves of totalitarianism" nor can officials have "absolute authority over their students," the Court solemnly concluded.

Quite possibly the principal in *Tinker* made an error in judgment. But by making matters of school discipline a constitutional issue, the Court has left educators fumbling their way through everyday disciplinary encounters with kids ever since. "At each elementary and middle school door, you have some guy making a constitutional decision every day," observes Jeff Krausman, legal counsel to several Iowa school districts. Suppose, says Krausman by way of example, that a student shows up at school wearing a T-shirt emblazoned WHITE POWER. The principal wants to send the kid home to change, but he's not sure it's within his authority to do so, so he calls the superintendent. The superintendent is also unsure, so he calls the district's lawyer. The lawyer's concern, though, isn't that the child has breached the boundaries of respect and tolerance, and needs an adult to tell him so, but whether disciplining the student would violate the First Amendment. Is this, in other words, literally a federal case?

And that's not easy to answer. "Where do you draw the line?" Krausman asks. "Some lawyers say you should have to prove that something is 'significantly disruptive.' But in Iowa you might have a hard time proving that a T-shirt saying WHITE POWER or ASIANS ARE GEEKS is significantly disruptive." Meanwhile, educators' power to instill civility and order in school dissolves into tendentious debates over the exact meaning of legal terms like "significantly disruptive."

In 1975 the Supreme Court hampered school officials' authority yet further in *Goss v. Lopez*, a decision that expanded the due process rights of students. *Goss* concerned several students suspended for brawling in the school lunchroom. Though the principal who suspended them actually witnessed the fight himself, the Court concluded that he had failed to give the students an adequate hearing before lowering the boom. Students, pronounced the Court, are citizens with a property right to their education. To deny that right requires, at the least, an informal hearing with notice, witnesses, and the like; suspensions for longer than ten days might require even more formal procedures.

Following *Tinker*'s lead, *Goss* brought lawyers and judges deeper inside the schoolhouse. You want to suspend a violent troublemaker? Because of *Goss*, you now had to ask: Would a judge find your procedures satisfactory? Would he agree that you have enough witnesses? The appropriate documentation? To suspend a student became a time-consuming and frustrating business.

Students soon learned that, if a school official does something they don't like, they can sue him, or at least threaten to do so. New York City special-ed teacher Jeffrey Gerstel's story is sadly typical. Last year Gerstel pulled a student out of his classroom as he was threatening to kill the assistant teacher. The boy collided with a bookcase and cut his back, though not badly enough to need medical attention. Even so, Gerstel found himself at a hearing, facing the student's indignant mother, who wanted to sue, and three "emotionally disturbed adolescents"—classmates of the boy—who witnessed the scuffle. The mother soon settled the dispute out of court and sent her son back to Gerstel's classroom. But by then Gerstel had lost the confidence he needed to handle a roomful of volatile teenagers, and the kids knew it. For the rest of the year they taunted him: "I'm going to get my mother up here and bring you up on charges."

In another typical recent case, a Saint Charles, Missouri, high schooler running for student council handed out condoms as a way of drumming up votes. The school suspended him. He promptly sued on free-speech grounds; in previous student council elections, he whined, candidates had handed out candy. Though he lost his case, his ability to stymie adults in such a matter, even if only temporarily, could not but give him an enlarged sense of his power against the school authorities: his adolescent fantasy of rebellion had come true.

These days, school lawyers will tell you, this problem is clearing up: in recent years, they point out, the courts have usually sided with schools in discipline cases, as they did in Missouri. But the damage done by *Tinker*, *Goss*, and their ilk isn't so easily undone. Lawsuits are expensive and time-consuming, even if you win. More important, the mere potential for a lawsuit shrinks the adult in the child's eyes. It transforms the person who should be the teacher and the representative of society's moral and cultural values into a civil servant who may or may not please the young, rights-armed citizen. The natural relationship between adult and child begins to crumble.

The architects of IDEA, *Tinker*, and *Goss*, of course, thought of themselves as progressive reformers, designing fairer, more responsive schools. Introducing the rights of free speech and due process, they imagined, would ensure that school officials would make fewer "arbitrary and capricious" decisions. But lawmakers failed to see how they were radically destabilizing traditional relations between adults and children and thus eroding school discipline.

School bureaucracies have struggled to restore the discipline that the courts and federal laws have taken away, but their efforts have only alienated students and undermined adult authority even more. Their first stratagem has been to bring in the lawyers to help them craft regulations, policies, and procedures. "If you have a law, you'd better have a policy," warns Julie Lewis, staff attorney for the National School Boards Association. These legalistic rules, designed more to avoid future lawsuits than to establish classroom order, are inevitably abstract and inflexible. Understandably, they inspire a certain contempt from students.

Putting them into practice often gives rise to the arbitrary and capricious decisions that lawmakers originally wanted to thwart. Take "zero tolerance" policies mandating automatic suspension of students for the worst offenses. These proliferated in the wake of Congress's 1994 Gun-Free Schools Act, which required school districts to boot out for a full year students caught with firearms. Many state and local boards, fearful that the federal law and the growing public clamor for safe schools could spawn a new generation of future lawsuits, fell into a kind of bureaucratic mania. Why not require suspension for *any* weapon—a nail file, a plastic Nerf gun? Common sense went out the window, and suspensions multiplied.

Other districts wrote up new anti-weapon codes as precise and defensive as any corporate merger agreement. These efforts, however, ended up making educators look more obtuse. When a New York City high school student came to school with a metal-spiked ball whose sole purpose could only be to maim classmates, he wasn't suspended: metal-spiked balls weren't on the superintendent's detailed list of proscribed weapons. Suspend him and he might sue you for being arbitrary and capricious.

Worse, the influence of lawyers over school discipline means that educators speak to children in an unrecognizable language, far removed from the straight talk about right and wrong that most children crave. A sample policy listed in "Keep Schools Safe," a pamphlet co-published by the National Attorneys General and the National School Boards Association (a partnership that itself says much about the character of American school discipline today), offers characteristically legalistic language: "I acknowledge and understand that 1. Student lockers are the property of the school system. 2. Student lockers remain at all times under the control of the school system. 3. I am expected to assume full responsibility for my school locker." Students correctly sense that what lies behind such desiccated language is not a moral worldview and a concern for their well-being and character but fear of lawsuits.

When educators aren't talking like lawyers, they're sounding like therapists, for they've called in the psychobabblers and psychologists from the nation's ed schools and academic departments of psychology to reinforce the attorneys in helping them reestablish school discipline. School bureaucrats have been falling over one another in their rush to implement trendy-sounding "research-based programs"—emotional literacy training, anti-bullying workshops, violence prevention curricula, and the like—as "preventive measures" and "early interventions" for various school discipline problems. Of dubious efficacy, these grimly utilitarian nostrums seek to control behavior in the crudest, most mechanical way. Nowhere is there any indication that adults are instilling in the young qualities they believe in and consider integral to a good life and a decent community. Kids find little that their innate sociality and longing for meaning can respond to.

Typical is "Second Step," a widely used safety program from a Seattle-based nonprofit. According to its architects, the goals of "Second Step" are "to reduce impulsive and aggressive behavior in children, teach social and emotional skills, and build self-esteem." Like many such therapeutic programs, it recommends role-playing games, breathing exercises, and learning to "identify feelings," "manage anger," and "solve problems." The universal moral values of self-control, self-respect, and respect for others shrink to mere "skills," as scripted and mechanical as a computer program.

In this leaden spirit, the National Association of School Psychologists newsletter, *Communiqué*, proposes a "Caring Habit of the Month Adventure," a program used by Aliquippa Middle School near Pittsburgh. Each month school officials adorn school hallways with posters and stickers that promote a different caring habit or "skill." The skittish avoidance of moral language is a giveaway: this is a program more in love with behavioral technique than inducting children into moral consciousness. It's not surprising to find that *Communiqué* recommends dedicating a month to each "skill," because "[r]esearchers say a month is about the length of time it takes to make a habit out of consistently repeated action."

The legal, bureaucratic, and therapeutic efforts make up what Senator McCain would call an "iron triangle," each side reinforcing the others. Consider the fallout from the Supreme Court's 1999 decision *Davis v. Monroe County School District*, which held that school districts could be liable for damages resulting from student-on-student sexual harassment. Now every school district in the country is preparing an arsenal to protect itself against future lawsuits: talking to lawyers, developing bureaucratic policies, and calling in therapeutic consultants or even full-time "gender specialists" to show a "proactive" effort to stamp out harassment. Experts at universities across the United States are contentedly churning out the predictable curricula, with such names as "Flirting and Hurting" and "Safe Date," as cloying and suspect to any normal adolescent as to a grownup.

The full consequence of these dramatic changes has been to prevent principals and teachers from creating the kind of moral community that is the most powerful and dependable guarantor of good discipline ever devised. When things work as they should—in the traditional manner familiar all over the world and across the ages—principals forge a cohesive society with very clear shared values, whose observance confers a sense of worth on all those who subscribe to them. People behave morally primarily because they assent to the standards of the group, not because they fear punishment. A community of shared values cannot be legalistic or bureaucratic or based on moronic behavior exercises; it must be personal, enforced by the sense that the authority figure is protective, benevolent, and worthy of respect.

That's why good principals have to be a constant, palpable presence, out in the hallways, in the classrooms, in the cafeteria, enforcing and modeling for students and staff the moral ethos of the school. They're there long before the school day begins and long after it ends; they know students' names, joke with them, and encourage them; and they don't let little things go—a nasty put-down between students, a profanity uttered in irritation, even a belt missing from a school uniform. They know which infraction takes only a gentle reminder and which a more forceful response—because they have a clear scale of values and they know their students. They work with their entire staff, from teachers to bus drivers, to enlist them in their efforts.

For such principals, safety is of course a key concern. Frank Mickens, a wonderful principal of a big high school in a tough Brooklyn neighborhood, posts seventeen staff members in the blocks near the school during dismissal time while he sits in his car by the subway station, in order to keep students from fighting and bullies from picking on smaller or less aggressive children. Such measures go beyond reducing injuries. When students believe that the adults around them are not only fair but genuinely concerned with protecting them, the school can become a community that, like a good family, inspires affection, trust—and the longing to please.

But how can you create such a school if you have to make students sit next to felons or a kid transferred to your school because he likes to carry a box cutter in his pocket? June Arnette, associate director of the National School Safety Center, reports that, after Columbine, her office received numerous e-mails from students who said they wouldn't bother reporting kids who had made threats or carried weapons because they didn't think teachers or principals would do anything about them. A number of studies show that school officials rarely do anything about bullies.

How can you convince kids that you are interested in their well-being when from day one of the school year you feel bureaucratic pressure to speak to them in legalistic or quasi-therapeutic gobbledygook rather than a simple, moral language they can understand? How can you inspire students' trust when you're not sure whether you can prevent a kid from wearing a WHITE POWER T-shirt or stop him from cursing at the teacher? It becomes virtually impossible, requiring heroic effort. Even when good principals come along and try to create a vibrant school culture, they are likely to leave for a new job before they have been able to effect change.

Since heroes are few, most principals tend to become what John Chubb and Terry Moe in *Politics, Markets and American Schools* call "lower-level managers," administering decisions made from above. Teachers often grumble that principals, perhaps enervated by their loss of authority, retreat into their offices, where they hold meetings and shuffle papers. It's not that they don't make a show of setting up "clear rules and expectations," as educators commonly call it, but they are understandably in a defensive mood. "Don't touch anyone. Mind your own business," was the way one New York City elementary school principal summed up her profound thinking on the subject.

In tough middle and high schools presided over by such functionaries, this defensive attitude is pervasive among teachers. "Protect yourself," one New York City high school teacher describes the reigning spirit. "If kids are fighting, stand back. Call a supervisor or a security guard. Don't get involved." That teachers are asked to rely for the safety of their students on security guards—figures unknown to schools thirty years ago—says much about the wreckage of both adult-child relations and of the school as a civil community. It also serves as a grim reminder that when adults withdraw from the thousand daily encouragements, reminders, and scoldings required to socialize children, authoritarian measures are all that's left.

The effect of the collapse of adult authority on kids is practically to guarantee their mistrust and alienation. Schools in this country, particularly high schools, tend to become what the sociologist James Coleman called an "adolescent society," dominated by concern with dating, sex, and consumerism. The loss of adult guidance makes it certain that adolescent society—more powerful than ever, if we're to believe recent TV shows like *Freaks and Geeks* and *Popular*—will continue in its sovereignty. Quaking before the threat of lawsuits and without support from their superiors, educators hesitate to assert the most basic civic and moral values that might pose a challenge to the crude and status-crazed peer culture. When they do talk, it is in a language that doesn't make any sense to kids and cannot possibly compel their respect.

Though under the current system it's easy to lose sight of this truth, there's nothing particularly complex about defining moral expectations for children. At one successful inner-city middle school I visited, a sign on the walls said, WORK HARD, BE KIND; BE KIND, WORK HARD: and if the school can instill just those two values, it will have accomplished about all we could ask. Educators who talk like this grasp that a coherent and meaningful moral environment is what socializes children best. Paul Vallas, as CEO of the Chicago public schools, introduced character education, community service requirements, and a daily recitation of the Pledge of Allegiance. "It's the Greek in me," explains Vallas. "I take Aristotle's approach to education. We are teaching kids to be citizens." Two and a half millennia later, Aristotle's approach remains a surer recipe for disciplined schools than all the belawyered conduct codes and all the trendy life-skills programs that the courts and the bureaucrats have given us.

[2000]

6

Tweens: Ten Going on Sixteen

During the past year my youngest morphed from child to teenager. Down came the posters of adorable puppies and the drawings from art class; up went the airbrushed faces of Leonardo DiCaprio and Kate Winslet. CDs of LeAnn Rimes and Paula Cole appeared mysteriously, along with teen fan magazines featuring glowering movie and rock-and-roll hunks with earrings and threatening names like Backstreet Boys. She started reading the newspaper—or at least the movie ads—with all the intensity of a Talmudic scholar, scanning for glimpses of her beloved Leo or, failing that, Matt Damon. As spring approached and younger children skipped past our house on their way to the park, she swigged from a designer-water bottle, wearing the obligatory tank top and denim shorts as she whispered on the phone to friends about games of Truth or Dare. The last rites for her childhood came when, embarrassed at reminders of her foolish past, she pulled a sheet over her years-in-the-making American Girl doll collection, now dead to the world.

So what's new in this dog-bites-man story? Well, as all

this was going on, my daughter was ten years old and in the fourth grade.

Those who remember their own teenybopper infatuation with Elvis or the Beatles might be inclined to shrug their shoulders as if to say, "It was ever thus." But this is different. Across class lines and throughout the country, elementary and middle school principals and teachers, child psychologists and psychiatrists, marketing and demographic researchers all confirm the pronouncement of Henry Trevor, middle school director of the Berkeley Carroll School in Brooklyn, New York: "There is no such thing as preadolescence anymore. Kids are teenagers at ten."

Marketers have a term for this new social animal, kids between eight and twelve: they call them "tweens." The name captures the ambiguous reality: though chronologically midway between early childhood and adolescence, this group is leaning more and more toward teen styles, teen attitudes, and, sadly, teen behavior at its most troubling.

The tween phenomenon grows out of a complicated mixture of biology, demography, and the predictable assortment of Bad Ideas. But putting aside its causes for a moment, the emergence of tweendom carries risks for both young people and society. Eight- to twelve-year-olds have an even more wobbly sense of themselves than adolescents; they rely more heavily on others to tell them how to understand the world and how to place themselves in it. Now, for both pragmatic and ideological reasons, they are being increasingly "empowered" to do this on their own, which leaves them highly vulnerable both to a vulgar and sensation-driven marketplace and to the crass authority of their immature peers. In tweens we can see the future of our society taking shape, and it's not at all clear how it's going to work.

Perhaps the most striking evidence for the tweening of

children comes from market researchers. "There's no question there's a deep trend, not a passing fad, toward kids getting older younger," says researcher psychologist Michael Cohen of Arc Consulting, a public policy, education, and marketing research firm in New York. "This is not just on the coasts. There are no real differences geographically." It seems my daughter's last rites for her American Girl dolls were a perfect symbol not just for her own childhood but for childhood, period. The Toy Manufacturers of America Factbook states that, where once the industry could count on kids between birth and fourteen as their target market, today it is only birth to ten. "In the last ten years we've seen a rapid development of upper-age children," says Bruce Friend, vice president of worldwide research and planning for Nickelodeon, a cable channel aimed at kids. "The twelve- to fourteen-year-olds of yesterday are the ten to twelves of today." The rise of the preteen teen is "the biggest trend we've seen."

Scorning any symbols of their immaturity, tweens now cultivate a self-image that emphasizes sophistication. The Nickelodeon-Yankelovich Youth Monitor found that by the time they are twelve, children describe themselves as "flirtatious, sexy, trendy, athletic, cool." Nickelodeon's Bruce Friend reports that by eleven, children in focus groups say they no longer even think of themselves as children.

They're very concerned with their "look," Friend says, even more so than older teens. Sprouting up everywhere are clothing stores like the chain Limited Too and the catalog company Delia, geared toward tween girls who scorn old-fashioned, little-girl flowers, ruffles, white socks, and Mary Janes in favor of the cool—black minidresses and platform shoes. In Toronto a tween store called Ch!ckaboom, which offers a manicurist and tween singing-star Jewel on the sound system, hypes itself as "an adventure playground where girls can hang out, have fun, and go nuts shopping." A recent article on tween fashion in the *New York Times* quoted one ten-year-old sophisticate primping in a changing room at Saks Fifth Avenue: "It's black and I love to wear black. It goes with everything."

Less cosmopolitan tweens may eschew the understated little black dress, but they are fashion-mad in their own way. Teachers complain of ten- or eleven-year-old girls arriving at school looking like madams, in full cosmetic regalia, with streaked hair, platform shoes, and midriff-revealing shirts. Barbara Kapetanakes, a psychologist at a conservative Jewish day school in New York, describes her students' skirts as being about "the size of a belt." Kapetanakes says she was told to dress respectfully on Fridays, the eve of the Jewish Sabbath, which she did by donning a long skirt and modest blouse. Her students, on the other hand, showed their respect by looking "like they should be hanging around the West Side Highway," where prostitutes ply their trade.

Lottie Sims, a computer teacher in a Miami middle school, says that the hooker look for tweens is fanning strong support for uniforms in her district. But uniforms and tank-top bans won't solve the problem of painted young ladies. "You can count on one hand the girls not wearing makeup," Sims says. "Their parents don't even know. They arrive at school with huge bags of lipstick and hair spray, and head straight to the girls' room."

Though the tweening of youth affects girls more visibly than boys, especially since boys mature more slowly, boys are by no means immune to these obsessions. Once upon a time, about ten years ago, fifth- and sixth-grade boys were about as fashion-conscious as their pet hamsters. But a growing minority have begun trading in their baseball cards for hair mousse and baggy jeans. In some places, two-hundred-dollar jackets, emblazoned with sports logos like the warm-up gear of professional athletes, are *de rigueur*; in others, the preppy look is popular among the majority, while the more daring go for the hipper style of pierced ears, fade haircuts, or ponytails. Often these tween peacocks strut through their middle school hallways taunting those who have yet to catch on to the cool look.

Cosmetics companies have found a bonanza among those we once thought of as children. Since the late fifties, the Tinkerbell Company has sold cosmetics to girls ages four to ten. For the most part, these were really more like toys, props for dress-up games and naive attempts to imitate Mommy. Today Tinkerbell has grown up and gone to Soho. New products for the spring of 1998 included roll-on body glitter and something called "hair mascara," a kind of roll-on hair color in what the company has described as "edgy colors"—neon green, bright blue, and purple. AM Cosmetics has introduced the Sweet Georgia Brown line for tweens. It includes body paints and scented body oils with come-hither names like Vanilla Vibe and Follow Me Boy. Thanks to the Cincinnati design firm Libby Peszyk Kattiman, after she has massaged her body with Follow Me Boy oil, your little darling will also be able to slip into some tween-sized bikini panties.

After completing her toilette, your edgy little girl might want to take in a movie with a baggy-panted, Niked dude. They won't bother with pictures aimed at them, though; nine to twelves are snubbing films like *Madeline* or *Harriet the Spy*. Edgy tweens want cool, hip, and sexy. "When I hear parents complain about no films for their young kids, it kind of gets to me," says Roger Birnbaum, producer of such films for preteens as *Angels in the Outfield* and *Rocket Man*, "because when you make those kinds of films, they don't take their kids to see them." They prefer R-rated films like *Object of My Affection*, about a young woman who falls in love with a homosexual; or *Scream*, the horror story about a serial killer hunting down young women; or the soap opera *Titanic*, which succeeded so hugely because teen and tween girls went back to watch three and a half hours of Leonardo DiCaprio three, four, even five times. "These are different times," concedes Stanley Jaffe, one of the producers of the new *Madeline*, in response to doubts about the potential of his movie, "and you can't go into it thinking you're making a children's film." In other words, there are no children's movies here.

The same goes for other media. Magazine publishers—by the early 1990s magazines like *Sports Illustrated for Kids* and *Nickelodeon* were beginning to replace comics as the print entertainment of choice for children—say that warm and cutesy images are out; cool is in. Celebrities like actor Will Smith and rapper Puff Daddy adorn the cover of almost every issue of *Nickelodeon*, the cable channel's magazine geared toward eight- to fourteen-year-olds. Editor Laura Galen says that whenever her magazine reduces its entertainment coverage, tween complaints flood the mail. By the late 1980s, tweens helped launch the new genre of what might be called peach-fuzz rock—bands made up of barely pubescent male sex-symbols-in-training. At that time girls were going screaming mad for a group called New Kids on the Block; after their voices changed and their beards grew in, New Kids lost out to a group called Hanson, which proceeded to fill stadiums with panting tweens.

Danny Goldberg, chief executive officer of Mercury Records, which produces Hanson, recalls that teen girls have had immense influence on the music business since the days of Frank Sinatra. "But now," he says, "the teenage years seem to start at eight or nine in terms of entertainment tastes. The emotions are kicking in earlier. It's a huge audience."

No aspect of children's lives seems beyond the reach of tween style. Even the Girl Scouts of America have had to change their image. In 1989 the organization commissioned a new MTV-style ad, with rap music and an appearance by tween lust-object Johnny Depp. Ellen Christie, a media specialist for the organization, said it had to "get away from the uniformed, goody-goody image and show that Girl Scouts are a fun, mature, cool place to be." The Girl Scouts?

Those who seek comfort in the idea that the tweening of childhood is merely a matter of fashion—who maybe even find their lip-synching, hip-swaying little boy or girl kind of cute—might want to think twice. There are disturbing signs that tweens are not only eschewing the goody-goody childhood image but its substance as well.

Tweens are demonstrating many of the deviant behaviors we usually associate with the raging hormones of adolescence. "Ninth and tenth grade used to be the starting point for a lot of what we call risk behaviors," says Brooklyn middle school head Henry Trevor as he traces the downward trajectory of deviancy many veteran educators observe. "Fifteen years ago they moved into the eighth grade. Now it's seventh grade. The age at which kids picture themselves starting this kind of activity has gone down."

Hard data about how tweens are defining deviancy down are sketchy. For one thing, most studies of risk behavior begin with fifteen-year-olds. High school kids give fairly reliable answers in surveys, but middle school kids are often confusingly inconsistent. As for ten-year-olds, until recently it seemed absurd for researchers to interview them about their sexual activity and drug use.

The clearest evidence of tweendom's darker side concerns crime. Although children under fifteen still represent a minority of juvenile arrests, their numbers grew disproportionately in the past twenty years. According to a report by the Office of Juvenile Justice and Delinquency Prevention, "offenders under age fifteen represent the leading edge of the juvenile crime problem, and their numbers are growing." Moreover, the crimes committed by younger teens and preteens are growing in severity. "Person offenses, which once constituted 16 percent of the total court cases for this age group," continues the report, "now constitute 25 percent." Headline grabbers—like Nathaniel Abraham of Pontiac, Michigan, an eleven-year-old who stole a rifle from a neighbor's garage and went on a shooting spree in October 1997, randomly killing a teenager coming out of a store; and eleven-year-old Andrew Golden, who, with his thirteen-year-old partner, killed four children and one teacher at his middle school in Jonesboro, Arkansas—are extreme, exceptional cases, but alas, they are part of a growing trend toward preteen violent crime.

Though the absolute numbers remain quite small, suicide among tweens more than doubled between 1979 and the mid-nineties. Less lurid but still significant, a London-based child advocacy group called Kidscape announced in March 1998 a 55 percent increase over the previous eighteen months in calls reporting tween girl-on-girl bullying, including several incidents involving serious injuries.

The evidence on tween sex presents a troubling picture too. Despite a decline among older teens for the first time since records have been kept, sexual activity among tweens increased during that period. It seems that kids who are having sex are doing so at earlier ages. Between 1988 and 1995 the proportion of girls saying they began sex before fifteen rose from 11 percent to 19 percent. (For boys, the number remained stable, at 21 percent.) This means that approximately one in five middle school kids is sexually active. Christie Hogan, a middle school counselor for twenty years in Louisville, Kentucky, says: "We're beginning to see a few pregnant sixth-graders." Many of the principals and counselors I spoke with reported a small but striking minority of sexually active seventh-graders.

Equally striking, though less easily tabulated, are other sorts of what Michael Thompson, an educational consultant and co-author of *Raising Cain: Protecting the Emotional Life of Boys*, calls "fairly sophisticated sexual contact" short of intercourse among tweens. Thompson hears from seventh- and eighth-graders a lot of talk about oral sex, which they don't think of as sex; "for them, it's just fooling around," he says. A surprising amount of this is initiated by girls, Thompson believes. He tells the story of a seventh-grade boy who had his first sexual experience when an eighth-grade girl offered to service him this way. "The boy wasn't even past puberty yet. He described the experience as not all that exciting but 'sort of interesting.'"

Certainly the days of the tentative and giggly preadolescent seem to be passing. Middle school principals report having to deal with miniskirted twelve-year-olds "draping themselves over boys" or patting their behinds in the hallways, while eleven-year-old boys taunt girls about their breasts and spread rumors about their own and even their parents' sexual proclivities. Tweens have even given new connotations to the word "playground": one fifth-grade teacher from southwestern Ohio told me of two youngsters discovered in the bushes during recess.

Drugs and alcohol are also seeping into tween culture. The past six years have seen more than double the number of eighth-graders who smoke marijuana (10 percent today) and those who no longer see it as dangerous. "The stigma isn't there the way it was ten years ago," says Dan Kindlon, assistant professor of psychiatry at Harvard Medical School and co-author with Michael Thompson of *Raising Cain*. "Then it was the fringe group smoking pot. You were looked at strangely. Now the fringe group is using LSD."

Aside from sex, drugs, and rock and roll, another teen problem—eating disorders—is also beginning to affect younger kids. This behavior grows out of premature fashion-consciousness, which has an even more pernicious effect on tweens than on teens, because, by definition, younger kids have a more vulnerable and insecure self-image. Therapists say they are seeing a growing number of anorexics and obsessive dieters even among late-elementary-school girls. "You go on Internet chat rooms and find ten- and eleven-year-olds who know every [fashion] model and every statistic about them," says Nancy Kolodny, a Connecticut-based therapist and author of *When Food's a Foe: How You Can Confront and Conquer Your Eating Disorder*. "Kate Moss is their god. They can tell if she's lost a few pounds or gained a few. If a powerful kid is talking about this stuff at school, it has a big effect."

What change in our social ecology has led to the emergence of tweens? Many note that kids are reaching puberty at earlier ages, but while earlier physical maturation may play a small role in defining adolescence down, its importance tends to be overstated. True, the average age at which girls begin to menstruate has fallen from thirteen to between eleven and twelve and a half today, but the very gradualness of this change means that twelve-year-olds have been living inside near-adult bodies for many decades without feeling impelled to build up a cosmetics arsenal or head for the bushes at recess. In fact, some experts believe that the very years that have witnessed the rise of the tween have also seen the age of first menstruation stabilize. Further, teachers and principals on the front lines see no clear correlation between physical and social maturation. Plenty of budding girls and bulking boys have not put away childish things, while an abundance of girls with flat chests and boys with squeaky voices ape the body language and fashions of their older siblings.

"Kids wear sexually provocative clothes at nine because their parents buy them provocative clothes, not because of their hormones," Robert L. Johnson, director of adolescent and young adult medicine at the University of Medicine and Dentistry of New Jersey, told me. "A lot of journalists call me to explain some of these things, and they want a good sound bite like 'raging hormones' rather than a complex series of social factors."

Of course the causes are complex, and most people working with tweens know it. In my conversations with educators and child psychologists who work primarily with middle-class kids nationwide, two major and fairly predictable themes emerged: a sexualized and glitzy media-driven marketplace and absentee parents. What has been less commonly recognized is that at this age the two causes combine to augment the authority of the peer group, which in turn both weakens the influence of parents and reinforces the power of the media. Taken together, parental absence, the market, and the peer group form a vicious circle that works to distort the development of youngsters.

Much of the media attention about parents working away from home for long hours has focused on infants and toddlers, but the effect of the postmodern domestic routine on a nine- or ten-year-old merits equal concern. The youngest children, after all, have continual adult attention, from baby-sitters or day-care attendants or after-school counselors. But as their children reach the age of eight or nine, many parents, after years of juggling schedules and panics over last-minute sore throats and stomachaches, breathe a sigh of relief as they begin to see growing signs of competence and common sense in their youngsters. Understandably concluding that their children are ready to take more responsibility for themselves, they place a list of emergency numbers on the refrigerator, arrange for a routine after-school phone call, and hand over the keys to the house.

In most people's minds, this sort of arrangement—children alone a few hours after school—is what we mean by latchkey kids. But latchkey kids come in many varieties. According to the educators I spoke with, many youngsters are leaving for school from an empty house after eating breakfast alone. Parents who can afford it will sometimes hand their children three dollars and tell them to pick up juice and a muffin on their way to school. Others have their children pick up fast food or frozen meals for dinner—which a small but sad minority will eat with only Bart Simpson or the local TV newscaster for company.

Almost without exception, the principals and teachers I spoke with describe a pervasive loneliness among tweens. "The most common complaint I hear," says Christie Hogan, "is, 'My mom doesn't care what I do. She's never home. She doesn't even *know* what I do.'" Although the loneliest and most estranged kids don't talk to counselors and can't even be coaxed into after-school programs when they are available, the more resourceful and socially well-adjusted children stay after school whether or not there is a formal program, hanging around popular teachers and counselors.

"We have to shoo them home at six sometimes," recounts one New York City middle school director. "They don't want to go home. No one's there."

Another, more subtly noxious consequence of the loss of family life has been less commonly understood: the expanding authority of a rigidly hierarchical and materialistic peer group. Kids, like nature, abhor a vacuum, and the power of the school peer group grows luxuriantly in soil left fallow by a rootless home life. With no one home, today's tween is captive to an age-segregated peer group whose inflexible customs and mall-driven ideals are too often the only ones he knows.

Many educators I talked with believe that kids are forming cliques earlier than ever, in the fifth and sixth grades rather than the seventh and eighth, as was the case until recently. Researchers are finding the same thing, as reported, for example, in a 1998 book entitled *Peer Power: Culture and Identity* by Patricia A. Adler with Peter Adler.

These peer groups should not be confused with simple childhood friendships. They are powerful and harsh mechanisms for making kids conform to the crudest, most superficial values. By late elementary school, according to *Peer Power*, boys understand that their popularity depends on "toughness, troublemaking, domination, coolness, and interpersonal bragging and sparring skills." Girls, on the other hand, "deriv[e] their status from their success at grooming, clothes, and other appearance-related variables; . . . [their] romantic success as measured through popularity and going with boys; affluence and its correlates of material possessions and leisure pursuits." Educators repeatedly note how harsh tweens are toward classmates who wear the wrong brand of sneakers or listen to yesterday's music. Childhood cruelty, always latent, finds an outlet in enforcing the rigid fashion laws of the in-group, whose dominion is now relatively unchallenged by parents and outside peers.

Paradoxically, then, while the tween has less company, he also has less privacy. Hannah Arendt once observed that if you think adults can be authoritarian in their dealings with children, you ought to see the peer group in action. Middle school can be a quasi-Orwellian world, where each child is under continual surveillance by his peers, who evaluate the way he walks, the way he looks, the people he talks to, the number of times he raises his hand in class, the grade he got on his science project. If two kids become romantically linked, their doings are communal property. Each phone call, kiss, or grope is reported, judged, and—in the case of boys, at any rate—simultaneously ridiculed and urged onward by the group leaders. "You kissing her?" they taunt, according to Patricia Hersch in her recent study entitled *A Tribe Apart.* "You get her in bed or something?" Not that things are better if you get rid of the boys. According to one fifth-grade teacher at a private New York City girls' school, students are frequently so wrought up about the vicissitudes of friendships within their group that they can't do their math or English.

Add to this hothouse a glamour- and celebrity-mad tween market culture, and things get even steamier. In fact both parental absence and the powerful peer group are intricately connected to the rise of a burgeoning tween market. To be sure, candy, toy, and cereal manufacturers had long known the power of tween cravings before they even defined this new niche group. But tweens really began to catch the eye of businesses around the mid-eighties, a time when, paradoxically, their absolute numbers were falling. The reason was simple. Market research began to reveal that more and more children this age were shopping for their own clothes, shoes, accessories, drugstore items—even for the family groceries.

Jordache Jeans was one of the first companies to spot the trend. "My customers are kids who can walk into a store with either their own money or their mothers'," explained the company's director of advertising at the time. "The dependent days of tugging on Mom or Dad's sleeve are over." Jordache celebrated the new era with ads befitting a revolution. Ignoring—or rather, scorning—parents, they appealed directly to kids who had money in their pockets and puerile dreams of sophistication in their heads. Parents found nothing amusing in seeing jeans-clad youngsters on TV, saying things like, "Have you ever seen your parents naked?" and "I hate my mother. She's prettier than me," and after many complaints, Jordache pulled the plug. Though today's tween ads downplay the shock effect, they take the same fundamental approach: kids are on their own, is the premise; flatter them as hip and aware almost-teens rather than out-of-it little kids—as independent, sophisticated consumers with their own language, music, and fashion.

Anyone who remembers high school will recall many of these dynamics. But it is important to recognize that the combination of isolation from adults, peer cruelty, and fantasies of sophistication, though always a danger to the alienated teenager, is especially taxing to the fragile ego of the preadolescent. With less life experience and even less self-awareness (if that's possible) than their teenage brothers and sisters, preadolescents have fewer internal resources to fall back on. As Helen Colvin, a middle school science teacher from Harrisburg, Pennsylvania, explains: "These kids have two years less time to become a firm person. That's two years less time to discover what they are, what they believe, to experiment with identity. Instead, they just want to be like their friends."

How do parents view all this? For while they may be out of the house for long hours, parents still have the capacity to break, or at least loosen, the choke hold of the peer group. Many parents negotiate diplomatic compromises, giving in on lipstick, say, while holding a line on pierced navels and quietly trying to represent alternatives. But a surprising number of parents, far from seeking to undermine their children's tweenishness, are enablers of it. When Jim Alloy, principal of Fox Lane Middle School in Bedford, New York, tried to ban tank tops, he was beset by a number of irate parents who accused him of discriminating against girls. Other educators marvel at the number of boys whose parents not only buy them expensive Starter jackets but immediately buy them another one if, as so often happens, they lose it.

Many parents are pleased to see their children hip to the market. "I'm glad my girls respond to fashion," said one mother of tweens in a recent *New York Times* article on tween fashion sense. "Trends aren't something you should learn about all of a sudden when you're in college." Another mother frowned over her seven-year-old's choice of a smocked dress as "too babyish." Nor does the enthusiasm for precocity stop with leopard-print tops and thigh-slit black skirts. I sat in amazement at a summer-camp performance one recent summer as a group of about thirty tweens sang a medley of rock-and-roll songs. The girls in their bare midriffs and miniskirts shimmied and vamped for the pleasure of their upper-middle-class parents, who whooped and hollered like revelers at a strip joint.

Of course, just because they like rock and roll doesn't mean these parents are trying to push their kids into sex and drugs or, for that matter, alcohol and anorexia. Doubtless many of them are panicky at the prospect of adolescence and all its dangers. Still, their enthusiasm for their children's pseudosophistication betrays a deep confusion about their own role.

The one theme that comes through loud and clear in talking to educators and therapists is that, with parents and their tween children, it's the blind leading the blind. "I'm hearing statements like, 'What can I do? I can't make him read,'" says one director of a New York City private middle school. "And the child is in fifth grade. What does it mean that an adult feels he cannot make a ten-year-old do something?" A middle school principal from Putnam County, New York, concurs: "I used to say to a kid behaving rudely, 'Young man, would you speak that way at home?' and he would hang his head and say, 'No.' Now I ask a kid, and he looks surprised and says, 'Yeah.'"

It's too simple to trace the trend toward passive parenting back to the time and energy deficits experienced by most working parents. The reluctance to guide and shape tween behavior is as much an ideological as a practical matter. Parents are suffering from a heavy diet of self-esteem talk. In their minds, to force a child to speak politely, to make him read, to punish him for being out of line, is to threaten his most primary need—to express himself. "You'll damage his self-esteem," principals and teachers often hear from parents of children who face discipline for troublemaking.

Though the most influential recent works on preteens and early adolescents, by feminist-inspired child specialists like Carol Gilligan and Peggy Orenstein, focus on girls, they capture the prevailing expert wisdom about self-esteem, whose sorry consequences can be seen in the boorish attitudes of both sexes. According to such experts, the biggest problem tween girls face is not a loss of adult guidance but the opposite. Parents and teachers are guilty of "silencing" girls around this age, goes the argument, and the result is a loss of self-confidence. Instead of submitting children to what Gilligan calls "the tyranny of the nice and the kind," adults should instead focus their parenting energies on supporting and modeling assertive behavior.

And Gilligan and her followers do mean assertive. The new model for girls is the sort of macho, braggart boy that in more levelheaded times made parents hide their daughters. In her study of several California middle schools, Orenstein is impressed by the self-confidence of the boys she observes who call out in class and shout one another down when they have an answer. "[W]hen the girls in [the] class do speak," she writes sadly, "they follow the rules."

Not only did these writers fail to think through what happens when adults believe that children are better off ignoring rules of behavior, but also they neglected to ask about the ultimate purpose of the power they proposed to hand over to children. Confidence, sure—but confidence in the service of what goal? Self-assertion toward what end? Kids certainly couldn't be expected to know the answer. There is nothing in the creed of self-esteem that encourages adults to help mold children's judgment about what matters in life. In fact, quite the opposite. Empowerment implies that children should determine their own style, codes of behavior, and values without serious interference from parents. And they have.

Though the experts missed it entirely, producers of popular culture have been quick to grasp the empty heart of child empowerment, just as they understood the related consequences of parental absence. They saw that children's will to power and immature longings were easy to exploit. Ad writers for Bonne Bell cosmetics, for instance, marry the approved language of self-esteem and the child's natural desire to seem grown-up and hip in the eyes of her peers. "We know how to be cool," goes the text accompanying pictures of a new product called Lip Lix. "We have our own ideas. And make our own decisions. Watch out for us. We are girls."

The Spice Girls, the wildly popular British rock singers who sported slip dresses, hot pants, belly shirts, and oily globs of lipstick and mascara, invented the term "girl power" precisely to evoke the empty formula of self-esteem, whose ingredients are nothing more than self-assertion and face paint—or nothing more than "strength, courage, and a Wonderbra," as one Spice Girl motto puts it. "I'll tell you what I want, what I really, really want," they sing in the tune familiar now to girls five years and older worldwide, girls who at concerts flash the Winston Churchill V sign and clench their fists in a power salute. And what is it? Caught up in the belief that power was in and of itself a satisfactory guiding virtue, self-esteem theorists failed to consider that what girls might really, really want is to dress up like female impersonators.

They also failed to grasp that empowerment is finally a greedy principle. When tweens talk about girl power on websites and in interviews, they make it clear that pure, undiluted self-esteem tends to ride roughshod over values smelling of self-restraint. "It's about not letting anyone judge you." "It's about no limitations," they write. *YM* magazine for teens has run a section called "Girl Zone: Your Guide to Kicking Butt."

Teachers confirm that, as far as kids are concerned, empowerment amounts to an in-your-face attitude. "If you tell them, 'You have to do your homework, or you won't graduate,'" says a counselor in a Queens middle school, "they look at you and say, 'So?'" A fifth-grade teacher at one East Side private girls' school says, "There's a lot of calling out. You try to get them to raise their hands, to wait their turn. They're very impatient and demanding. They challenge every point on the test. They insist on attention immediately." In Hollywood it is said that tweens roar with pleasure when the *Titanic* character played by Kate Winslet tells her mother to shut up and punctuates her order with an obscene gesture.

Of course, girls are not the only beneficiaries of the ideology of child empowerment. Boys also are enjoying the reign of "no limitations." Faced with students who have been taught the lessons of their own empowerment and who have no experience of authoritative, limit-setting adults at home, educators find themselves coping with a growing indifference toward authority. It's a situation the schools have trouble handling. When they want to discipline boys who are caught writing obscenities in a girl's yearbook, or stuffing a backpack down the toilet, or throwing a stink bomb in the school auditorium—to cite a few of the examples I heard—school officials are not likely to receive any support from the parent. Seeing their job as being their child's advocate in the narrowest, legalistic sense, parents of the culprits in these instances cajoled, manipulated, and argued against any attempt by the school to have their sons face the music.

It is likely that girls' traditional role as goody-goodies used to act as a brake on boys' natural tendency toward restlessness and machismo. Now, as girls are "empowered" to become as bad as they wanna be, boys are "empowered" to become even badder. "Sixth-graders used to be benign and afraid of adults," Bedford, New York, principal Jim Alloy told me. "Now you see some of them who are so defiant, their parents have no idea what to do with them. I have several students from affluent homes with PINS petitions against them." (PINS, which stands for Person in Need of Supervision, allows local authorities to intercede with out-of-control kids.) Whether boy or girl, empowered children, it seems, find support for—or at least, indifference toward—their worst impulses.

Thus tweens, far from being simply a marketing niche group, speak to the very essence of our future. They are the vanguard of a new, decultured generation, isolated from family and neighborhood, shrugged at by parents, dominated by peers, and delivered into the hands of a sexualized and status- and fad-crazed marketplace.

A second-grade teacher told me that, at her school's yearly dance festival, she is finding it increasingly difficult to interest her seven-year-olds in traditional kid stuff like the Mexican hat dance or the hokey-pokey. They want to dress up like the Spice Girls and shimmy away. Look for the tweening of America to continue its downward march.

[1998]

7

What's Wrong with the Kids?

On April 20, 1999, two seemingly ordinary boys from normal middle-class families walked into their high school in an affluent suburb of Denver and shot and killed twelve of their classmates and a teacher before finally turning their guns on themselves. It was a watershed moment in contemporary American life, a definitive fall from innocence that made parents and teachers look on their kids with unfamiliar feelings of anxiety and doubt. There had been other school shootings, of course, but Columbine—the name itself quickly settled into the lexicon—tapped far more deeply into a lurking fear that even during the unprecedentedly good times of the 1990s something might be going wrong with the nation's kids.

What troubled Americans about Columbine was the combination of the extraordinarily willful viciousness of the massacre and the very ordinary middle-classness of its perpetrators and its setting. One could explain violence in inner-city schools: poverty and urban crime had been intertwined since the days of Dickens's London. And, though no one might say it out loud, many Americans could pass over a school shooting in Jonesboro, Arkansas, or West Paducah, Kentucky, without too much comment. The folk in the hills and hollers, Mark Twain taught the nation, can sometimes be a little irrational.

But Columbine was different. Columbine made us wonder if we had been in denial about some sickness at the heart of the middle-class culture that most American kids know as reality. "Where were the parents?" many people asked, bewildered at how two teenagers could build up an arsenal in their own bedrooms without their mother or father knowing. "What kind of schools have we created?" others wonder on hearing that the two were making videos and writing essays for school about their vile fantasies without anyone being particularly impressed.

In the fall of 1999, stories from two unlikely (because relentlessly conventional) sources, PBS's *Frontline* and *Time* magazine, began to give us an answer to these questions. By entering deeply into the daily lives of American middle-class children as they interact with their families and schools, the stories offer some real insight into the roots of the teen alienation and emptiness that culminated in Columbine. They add up to a devastating portrait of *adults*, who were not neglectful or abusive in any conventional sense, but who, apart from lavish houses and abundant entertainment, have nothing of substance to pass on to children. Without the producers and writers fully understanding what they have uncovered, their portrait reinforces the suspicion that Columbine may reflect a spiritual and emotional void within contemporary American middle-class culture, into which troubled teenagers can easily pour their most grotesque and often rage-filled fantasies.

The adults who appear in the first and most important of these portraits, "The Lost Children of Rockdale County," which aired on the PBS series *Frontline*, would seem to have everything to offer children. About twenty-five miles east of Atlanta, Rockdale is Littleton's sociological twin, a booming, affluent suburb—"the fastest-growing settlement in human history," according to some locals quoted on the show. As is the case with Littleton, many Rockdale residents are new-comers to the region who have succeeded in their search for the good life. We get innumerable images of the wide streets of pristine subdivisions and newly sprouted McMansions, with their cathedral ceilings and airy, granite-countered kitchens. And, in fact, the mothers and fathers who inhabit these perfect houses do a good deal of what we hear good parents today ought to do: they coach Little League teams, they go on family vacations, they fix dinner for the kids. In the end, though, they remain utterly clueless when it comes to turning their mansions into homes where children can learn how to lead meaningful lives. Devoid of strong beliefs, seemingly bereft of meaningful experience to pass on to their young, they have at their center a vague emptiness that comes to seem the exact inverse of the meticulous opulence of their homes. The *Frontline* episode could just have easily been titled "The Lost Adults of Rockdale County."

The occasion for the show was an outbreak of syphilis that ultimately led health officials to treat two hundred teenagers. What was so remarkable was not that two hun-dred teenagers in a large suburban area were having sex and had overlapping partners. It was the way they were having sex. This was teen sex as *Lord of the Flies* author William Golding might have imagined it, a heart-of-darkness tribal rite of such degradation that it makes a collegiate "hook-up" look like splendor in the grass. Group sex was commonplace, as were thirteen-year-old participants. Kids would watch the Playboy cable TV channel and make a game of imitating everything they saw. They tried almost every permutation of sexual activity imaginable—vaginal, oral, anal, girl on girl, several boys with a single girl, or several girls with a boy. (The only taboo was homosexual activity among boys.) During some drunken parties, one girl might be "passed around" in a game. A number of the kids had upward of fifty partners. Some kids engaged in what they called a "sandwich"—while a girl performs oral sex on one boy, she is penetrated vaginally by another boy and anally by yet another.

According to the producers, it was the profound loneliness of these children that led them to seek a "surrogate family" in the company of their peers. No one could dispute that these children were lonely. Some were the virtual orphans of broken and dysfunctional homes. Others were simply the children of part-time parents, who were out of the house working long hours to provide their children with lavish homes, cars, cell phones, and the latest teen fashions. Most of the sex parties took place after school, between 3 p.m. and 7 p.m., in houses emptied of working adults. Other times, kids slipped out of the house after midnight without waking their exhausted parents.

But it gradually becomes clear that the absence in these kids' lives is not limited to office hours, and the loneliness they suffer goes beyond being left alone. Their parents, even when at home, seem disconnected. As the producers see it, one of the problems is that these families spend most of their time, including meals, in front of the television. "You just go fix your plate, eat, watch TV, finish watchin' whatever you're watchin'," one girl explains. The camera follows a boy named Kevin as he shuffles from the kitchen (with television, of course) out to his bedroom in the family pool house, where he has, inexplicably, *two* televisions, both enormous, and both flickering at the time of his interviews. In fact, the television is on in the background during a number of the show's home interviews, a detail that turns out to be more than local color. A Kaiser Foundation study released shortly after the "The Lost Children of Rockdale County" aired found that two-thirds of children have televisions in their rooms and that 58 percent of parents admitted that the TV was on during dinner.

Yet surely a diet of *The Simpsons* and *Dawson's Creek* is more a symptom than a cause of middle-class ills. The truth is, though the show's creators can't quite put their finger on the problem, these shadowy adults have removed themselves from the universal task of parenthood: that is, guiding and shaping the young. And they have done so not because they are too busy at work or watching television but because they have no cultural tools with which to do their jobs. They know they must love their children; they know they must provide for them—both of which they can do abundantly. The producers are clearly and rightly critical of the way these adults have translated material goods into the sum and substance of parental obligation. But when it comes to the cultural resources that would outfit their children with the moral awareness and worthy aspirations that would help them form a firm sense of self, these parents are deeply impoverished. Here the producers can only make some ineffectual speculation.

Yet the producers' inability to define this scarcity is as important a part of the Rockdale story as the sex parties and syphilis outbreak, for it reflects a more general confusion about the cultural impoverishment suffered by many children today. The profile of one father and daughter in particular dramatizes how the Rockdale parents and the media are similarly befuddled. Amy, a soft-spoken and pallid young woman, who smiles shyly as she tells her story, clearly has had all the benefits of a privileged childhood. We see shots from the family videos and photo albums—doubtless made by parents bursting with pleasure—of the braided girl whacking a ball during a Little League game, grinning sweetly as she carries her Easter basket in her pretty party dress, and nestling happily in the lap of her contentedly smiling father. In fact Amy's father did everything the books tell you to do. (Amy's mother refused to be interviewed.) He coached her baseball team; the family went on vacations together; he appears to have good reason to say, "We were close." But—he finally admits, in what appears to be a moment of revelation—they watched too much television. "We've got TVs in every room in the house," he says. "I watch my programs. My wife watches her programs. . . . Much of the time we had together was not together." Pressed, he says forlornly, "I guess we should have talked more."

Can this really explain how this spunky, beloved little girl became a teenager so desperately lonely that, urged on by two boys, she engaged in rough sex in front of her terrified three-year-old nephew and that she allowed herself to be used as a ferry service by "friends" whom she sensed liked her only "because she had a car"? It seems we are to believe so. During another scene, a health expert tells, with heartfelt frustration we are evidently supposed to share, about the reaction of the families of Rockdale when she speaks at a public meeting about the syphilis epidemic. A minister had turned to her and exclaimed about the parents: "Don't they see? Don't they see it's *them*? They don't talk to their children!" This insight is certainly consistent with prevailing expert wisdom. The Kaiser Foundation, in conjunction with Children Now, for instance, has begun a campaign entitled "Talking with Kids About Tough Issues," which implies that the problem facing adults today is that they are failing "to impart their own values and, most importantly, to create an atmosphere of open communication with their children on any issue."

But while it goes without saying that parents should talk to their children and "impart their own values"—is there anyone who believes they shouldn't?—this advice begs the obvious question: What exactly is it they are supposed to say? What values are they supposed to impart? To this question, no one—neither the Kaiser Foundation nor the *Frontline* producers—dares venture an answer. Should they tell their children it's not a good idea for them to be having sex with forty partners? Why not? Because they might get syphilis, or because it violates all sense of dignity and modesty? Should they recommend their child see a therapist? A minister? A gynecologist? An expert on Tantric sex? It doesn't seem to matter as long as they're talking and expressing their "values." Talking and imparting values show that adults are "caring."

Yet the *Frontline* producers unwittingly lead us to the conclusion that adults are not talking to their children for the same reason experts themselves can only deliver these platitudes. They don't believe there are any firm values to impart. These parents undoubtedly do not approve of group sex or sexually transmitted diseases or, for that matter, shooting one's classmates. But they have absorbed from the surrounding culture an ethos of nonjudgmentalism, which has drained their beliefs on these matters of all feeling and force. This suspension of all conviction helps explain the bland, sad air of many of these interviews. "They have to make decisions, whether to take drugs, to have sex," the mother of Kevin, the boy who lives in the pool house, intones expressionlessly. "I can give them my opinion, tell them how I feel. But they have to decide for themselves." It's hard to see how imparting her values will do anything to help her child. After all, these values have no gravity or truth. They are only her opinion.

The children of Rockdale know full well that their parents have nothing to say to them. "In my family, you do what you want to do. No one is going to stop you," Kevin says factually, without a hint of rebellion or arrogance. True, his mother did at one time attempt to be a parent to Kevin's older sister but gave up because she found "it was easier to let her [do what she wanted]. We got along better." Convinced that there are no values worth fighting for, the lost adults of Rockdale County have abdicated the age-old distinction between parents and children and have settled for being their children's friends and housemates. "We're pretty much like best friends or something," one girl said of her parents. "I mean, I can pretty much tell 'em how I feel, what I wanna do, and they'll let me do it." "I don't really consider her a mom all that much," another girl agrees about her own mother. "She takes care of me and such, but I consider her a friend more."

When adults turn into friends, childhood must disappear. Childhood cannot exist with no adults around. The children of Rockdale, still baby-faced and restlessly energetic, have lost all the sense of wonder, spontaneity, and idealism that we ordinarily associate with childhood. One of the most memorable images from the documentary is of three cherubic fourteen-year-olds demonstrating their sexual activities with the stuffed animals that still lie heaped on the bed in one of their rooms. It is in this child's bedroom, whose walls are decorated with graffiti, some of it obscene, that they also chant the lyrics of their favorite rap song: "He can get the bitch fucked, but how many can get the dick sucked," goes one of the lines. The tone of their delivery is a mixture of robotic chanting and giggling, and it captures perfectly the pathetic struggle inside them between the nihilisms their own degraded experience has taught them and the childishness that nature insists still defines them.

For nihilism, as Columbine seems to have taught us, is the eventual outcome for that considerable number of children today who are growing up deprived of any inherited wisdom about the longings and limits of human nature. Left to feel their way through life by themselves, they will inevitably stumble into experiences against which they have no defenses, experiences that will ultimately leave them numb. One thinks of Heather, who by the time she was twelve was left by her single mother to fend for herself for a week at a time when the mother was away on business trips. The child turned to alcohol and drugs and one day woke up to realize she had been raped while she was passed out. Her own words offer a sad epigraph on the weightless life to which she was abandoned. "The first time that you have sex, you think it's 'cause it means something," she says at fourteen. "But then you realize it doesn't. You just don't really care anymore."

Among her peers, even the reality of a serious disease becomes nothing to get excited about. Taking her daughter to the county health office to be tested for syphilis, one mother assumed the girl would be chastened. Not at all. The kids laughed and gave each other the high-five. "We thought it was funny," one girl said of the occasion. "'Oooh, you got syphilis,' you know. . . . It was like the cooties game little kids play, you know." These children's deadened sensibilities leave them incapable of horror—and, for all their sexual adventures, of pleasure. "Sex sucks, actually," says another. "I think sex was made for guys, because you just lay there, and you're just like, 'Get off me, what are you doing?'"

What's Wrong with the Kids?

A month to the day after Columbine, Rockdale County was the scene of another school shooting, when a fifteen-year-old sophomore opened fire and wounded six people at Heritage High School, where some of the kids interviewed by *Frontline* were enrolled. T. J. Solomon, the boy who committed the crime, was said to be depressed. After watching "The Lost Children of Rockdale County," one can begin to understand why.

Of course it would be oversimplifying things to blame parents for the ills of children like those of Rockdale and leave it at that. Parents are not some subculture with its own belief-system and habits; they are citizens of a wider culture, and in their child-rearing practices they are conforming to its demands. An October 1999 cover story in *Time*, entitled "A Week in the Life of a High School: What It's Really Like Since Columbine," illustrates that culture at work inside our educational institutions. *Time* chose to base its diary on Webster Groves High School in Webster Groves, Missouri—a town of about 23,000, ten miles southwest of St. Louis—precisely because it struck them as so ordinary. (In fact CBS chose Webster Groves to be the subject of a 1966 documentary for the same reason.) Indeed, as in Littleton and Rockdale, it is the ordinariness of Webster Groves that makes its story so troubling.

Like the lost adults of Rockdale County, Webster Groves's educators have also disengaged themselves from the task of shaping and training the young. And like Rockdale parents, they view the cultural heritage that might transform these youngsters into morally aware, aesthetically and intellectually alert adults as optional, a matter of opinion rather than of firmly held conviction. Thus the few ambitious college-bound students of Webster Groves may choose to read serious literature and do serious math. But those who don't feel like it—that is, the large majority—can choose to remain in their complacent, uncultivated state. The effect is to turn the institution into day care for teenagers, a high school baby-sitting service to keep kids off the streets. Students can satisfy the most challenging requirement, English (or "communication skills," as the school gratingly calls it), for instance, by taking journalism courses or a children's literature class, in which they read books by Dr. Seuss and other works written at the third-grade level or below. Or they might take a dumbed-down tenth-grade English class. On the day the *Time* writers visited, this class was analyzing a short story called "Sweet Potato Pie." The teacher describes eating sweet potato pie, ham hocks, collard greens. "And what do all these things have in common?" the teacher challenges her group of fifteen-year-old students. "They don't care if you learn," says one junior boy astutely. "They only care if you pass."

It could be argued that, unlike the parents of Rockdale County, Webster Groves educators have a good excuse for their surrender. State officials have made it clear that they view teaching students as secondary to educators' central task: to keep kids from dropping out and becoming social menaces. The state of Missouri gives bonus money to schools that have been able to reduce their dropout rate, and in Webster Groves that has amounted to $150,000, an irresistible sum considering that the school is staring at a $1.2 million deficit. Yet these funds also turn out to give students a way to blackmail teachers. Not only does the attendance bonus force teachers to dumb down the curriculum—"you promise not to ask us to read anything above a sixth-grade level, and we'll promise to stay in school" is the unspoken bargain—it also renders them powerless to enforce discipline against all but the most threatening infractions. Students can curse at teachers and saunter in late to class without penalty; teachers know the administration can't do much to back them up.

Most of the faculty has also stopped assigning more than fifteen minutes of homework a night. One teacher estimates that only 15 percent of her class does the work she assigns, and kids report doing ten minutes, thirty minutes a night, tops. ("They're safe here, and they can learn in class, even if they aren't doing homework," an assistant principal explains.) And teachers assign little homework, so that kids have plenty of time to do what they really want to do: make money. Students commonly work thirty or even forty hours a week in bagel or video stores—not to save up for college but to buy four-hundred-dollar leather jackets and cool cars whose central importance in life their education does nothing to challenge.

In Webster Groves, as in Rockdale, adults who have surrendered any semblance of the authority that normally invests those of greater experience and understanding try to disguise their negligence by pretending they are their charges' friends and peers. The *Time* article opens when the principal arrives for a predawn workout in a Goofy T-shirt, and her garb sets the tone of much that follows. Two teachers frequently engage in practical jokes, such as shooting Super Soaker water guns at students from the roof, a prank that led a frightened neighbor who could only see their outlines to call the police. The week that *Time* visited the school, the two climbed up to the roof again, this time to dangle the head of a female mannequin they'd named Headrietta so that it hangs in front of a classroom window and elicits the screams of female students. Comments *Time* about one of the zany pair: "It's hard to tell whether Yates, physics and astronomy teacher and chair of the science department, is a member of the faculty or still a kid." Yates's strenuous efforts to keep things friendly don't always work. His students continue to "dis" him or call him "asshole," behavior that Yates reassures himself is a sign that they are "comfortable" with him.

Extreme as it is, Yates's evasion is the way many adults today tell themselves that they are doing well by the young. As long as the kids stay in school, as long as their self-esteem is unthreatened, as long as the adult-child friendship appears relatively trouble-free, they can tell themselves they have a "good relationship with the kids." Indeed, the writers of "A Week in the Life" depict the educators of Webster Groves as caring adults who put in extra time going to school football games and playing in faculty-student softball competitions as well as reaching out to a teen whose mother just died or another whose parents are getting divorced.

But none of this can fill the void left by their own failure, and doubtless that of most of their students' parents, to represent a coherent moral and intellectual order. One of the main jobs of the educators of Webster Groves is to manage the decline brought about by their own abdication. Though the school has no guards or metal detectors, the principal and her assistants, including a detective, wander the halls between classes with walkie-talkies. Officials installed costly tracer equipment on the school telephone after a bomb scare last year. The faculty has crisis management seminars for working out responses to hypothetical emergencies. The school keeps a wary eye on the many kids on medication, and teachers are on the alert for those who suddenly lose interest in activities or whose grades decline.

Erik Erikson once defined adulthood as a period of generativity, when the mature nurture the vulnerable young and prepare them for independent life. What the stories from both *Frontline* and *Time* suggest is that in many parts of

What's Wrong with the Kids?

America adulthood in this sense has vanished. Adults have no meaningful cultural nourishment for filling the empty imaginations of their children, nothing to give order to their chaotic, unformed selves. For middle-class kids, a generation richer than any in human history, the predicament is grim. Setting out on the search for human meaning, they see adults staring vacantly at the ground.

It's enough to make some of them pretty mad.

[2000]

8

The L Word: Love as Taboo

I can see no trace of the passions which make for deeper joy," wrote Stendhal about Americans in his 1822 essay "Love." "It is as if the sources of sensibility have dried up among these people. They are just, they are rational, and they are not happy at all." Imagine the Frenchman's horror if he could hear today's Americans speak of *l'amour* in what *Mademoiselle* magazine calls this "Post-Idealist, Neo-Pragmatic Era of Relationships." Here is Wanda Urbanska, author of *The Singular Generation*, describing her peers in their twenties: "We . . . do not have affairs, we have 'sexual friendships.' We do not fall in love, we build relationships. We do not date, we 'see' each other." A student quoted in an article in the *Vassar Quarterly* adopts the same cool attitude. She doesn't care for the term *boyfriend* or *lover*; she speaks instead of "my special friend with whom I spent lots of quality physical time."

Many critics of popular culture decry its heat. But oddly enough, the familiar displays of sex and violence often go hand in hand with a distinct lowering of the emotional temperature. We are rarely moved by them—and neither are our heroes or stars. They display cool, tough self-sufficiency in each chiseled muscle and sneering put-down. Sure, the bed-hopping may seem sexy at first, but before long its vacant predictability adds up to a big yawn.

Even rock and roll, once a soulful forum for aching, lonely hearts or ecstatic lovers, is now just as likely to rap or croon a message of tough, don't-need-nobody independence. "You gotta be bad," sings Des'ree in a top-ten hit; "you gotta be strong; you gotta be hard; you gotta be tough; you gotta be stronger; you gotta be cool." Her counsel finds visual embodiment in fashion ads, such as that for Calvin Klein One unisex perfume—perfume, of all things, the primal sexual lure!—in which a line of grungy young men and women demonstrate, with snarling mouths and pointed fingers, various permutations of seen-it-all exasperation.

The emotional coolness and self-sufficiency of the Neo-Pragmatic Era of Relationships often finds much more easy-going expression than this. Television comedian Jerry Seinfeld portrays the benign, loopy side of casual sexual friendships in his top-rated series. He, his eccentric buddies, and Elaine, an ex-lover who seems more like his twin sister, drift good-naturedly through a landscape of sexual friendships that inspire about the same level of feeling as the tuna sandwiches Jerry's friend George orders at the local coffee shop. In the 1992 movie *Singles*, the theme song, "Dyslexic Heart," evokes the sad confusion of the young and disconnected. "For some people, living alone is a nasty hang," shrugs Cliff, one of the movie's slacker heroes, to a girl unaccountably and unsuccessfully pursuing him. "Not me. I'm a self-contained unit."

Of course it would be absurd to suggest that romantic love is dead in America. After all, for every *Seinfeld* there's a *Mad About You*, a comedy series about a devoted newlywed couple. And for every Des'ree there's a Beverly DeAngelis, a romance guru who writes self-help best-sellers with titles like *Are You the One for Me?*

Still, if love in America is not dead, it is ailing. It is suffering from the phenomenon the historian Peter Stearns describes in his book *American Cool*. American cool disdains intense emotions like grief, jealousy, and love, which leave us vulnerable, in favor of an "emotional style" of smooth detachment. If pop-culture gods present an elegant vision of American cool, for ordinary mortals the picture is less glamorous. But the unintended consequences of this banal ideal are the same across the economic spectrum: emotional frustration, alienation, and a sexual scene that recalls the drearier imaginings of Nietzsche or Freud.

American cool goes hand in hand with a profoundly rationalistic vision of human relations, which looks with suspicion on mystery, myth, and strong feeling. Powerful cultural trends have combined to produce this general coarsening and flattening of the sensibilities: feminism, which feared that love and equality were incompatible; the scientific rationalism of experts from the helping professions, who have helped advance what Lionel Trilling called our "commitment to mechanical attitudes toward life"; and, above all, America's fierce individualism, whose ideal is the free and adventurous loner.

The beginnings of the disenchantment of love and the rise of American cool are well worth examining if only to gauge the trade-offs we have made during this era of liberation. We've purchased our freedom from inhibition and guilt with a loan from imagination and fantasy. And to gain the array of pleasure once denied the bourgeois soul, we've paid the price of deep feeling.

Feminists mounted the first significant challenge to love's

hold on the American imagination. Romantic love is a myth, they argued, a myth inextricably tied up with women's inequality. It reinforced the idea of separate spheres for the sexes, providing a "consolation," as writer Juliet Mitchell put it, for women's "confinement in domesticity." Further, feminists contended, the ideal of love strengthens the myth of weak, dependent womanhood in need of strong male protection. Though this view got some airing as early as the mid-nineteenth century, it took on angry, raw urgency in the early 1970s in works like Shulamith Firestone's *The Dialectic of Sex* and Marilyn French's *The Women's Room*, which called love a "lie to keep women happy in the kitchen so they won't ask to do what men are always doing." Ti-Grace Atkinson went even further: "The psychopathological condition of love is a euphoric state of fantasy in which the victim transforms her oppressor into the redeemer. ... Love has to be destroyed." Not just a myth and a dangerous illusion, love was a disease in need of a cure.

Some Victorian feminists offered a cure, or at least an antidote, in the form of what they called "rational love." They advocated an "educated" or "organized" union between men and women, a union based on mutual interests and friendly companionship, with knowledge replacing fantasy and reason superseding untidy passions like jealousy and obsession. In a similar vein, feminists in the 1920s supported the introduction of college marriage courses aimed at dispelling romantic myths with objective, expert knowledge. Companionate marriage—cemented with shared interests, common background, and sexual pleasure rather than strong emotion—became the new rational ideal.

A health and family-life curriculum from the New Jersey Coalition for Battered Women exemplifies a contemporary version of this ideal. The curriculum sets up a contrast between bad, illusory "romantic love" and good, clearheaded "nurturing love." The latter entails responsibility, sharing, friendship, pleasure, and "strong feelings." But examples of "What Love Isn't" include jealousy, possessiveness, obsession, dependency, and giving yourself up—that is, just about every extreme of feeling that romantic love may arouse.

The feminist view of the myth of love contained a curious, counterproductive misreading of history. For if love served to subjugate women, it did no less to men. In many countries where romantic love has not been institutionalized, men's philandering is winked at while respectable women are kept veiled and hidden. In its first institutional flowering in the guise of medieval courtly love, stylized passion turned the wandering, brutish young men of the day—who might literally rape an unprotected woman as easily as slay that night's dinner—into sensitive, pining poets. The important point altogether ignored by early progressive reformers and feminists was that it was precisely as a powerful way of sublimating the passions that romantic love was a civilizing force. A man in love was a man subdued.

But a man in rational or nurturing love? As Peter Stearns points out, the changing articles of *Esquire* magazine suggest just how compelling men would find "organized," "educated" sharing. In the 1930s *Esquire* endorsed the new companionate marriage recommended by feminists and sociologists, publishing many stories and advice columns exploring what one writer called "Brave New Love" and cautioning against the excesses of romantic passion. But by World War II the magazine, presaging the arrival of *Playboy*, dispensed with all love talk and got down to the nitty-gritty: sex. *Esquire*'s trajectory from love to brave new love to sex suggested that lifting the veil of the illusion of love might reveal not the sweet smile of equal, harmonious sexual relations but the predacious grin of raw impulse.

Doctors and health experts, starting at the turn of the century, espoused theories that echoed the feminist disdain for passion and fantasy. Inspired by advances in the understanding and treatment of venereal disease, the medical profession argued against Victorian sexual repressiveness and in favor of a demystification of sex. "Sex mystery prevents progress," announced a book by a social hygienist, as progressive reformers devoted to the eradication of venereal disease called themselves. By releasing "sex mystery" from the murky control of priests and superstition and bringing it under the bright light of science, humanity would enjoy health and progress.

For all their innovativeness, the social hygienists were hardly sexual freethinkers; by and large they believed in the Victorian virtues of chastity and self-restraint. But they began a process of the medicalization and rationalization of sex whose basic assumptions continue to control much current thinking on the subject. They believed that sexual desire could yield easily to the discipline of logic and information; hence they became the first to advocate sex education in the schools. They would probably not be surprised to find that today it is still usually taught in health classes. And they introduced what author Barbara Dafoe Whitehead has called the "Scopes-trial terms" that continue to make the sex education debate so stubbornly hyperbolic: the scientifically minded, enlightened realists versus the superstitious, religious flat-earthers.

Yet the social hygienists would surely be dismayed by some of what is done in the name of health today. For the idea of rationalized and demystified sex has been stretched to its logical limits, as sex mystery—the dense subject of poets, philosophers, mystics, lyricists, and sacred codes— has given way to sex mechanics.

Nowhere is this robotization of sex more glaring than in the curricula of modern sex educators, the intellectual heirs of the social hygienists. In what may have been a swan song of sexual love in 1959, a sex education manual began: "The end and aim of sex education is developing one's fullest capacity for love." Today nothing could seem more quaint. Most modern sex education programs center on teaching not just health but technical skills—communication skills, decision-making skills, refusal skills, and, of course, condom skills. Some years ago the Massachusetts Department of Public Health produced an AIDS-prevention video in which a hip young nurse distributes flash cards depicting the fourteen stages of condom use. The students get together, look at one another's cards, and decide the proper order—which looks like this: "Talk with Partner," "Decision by Both Partners to Have Sex," "Buy the Condom," "Sexual Arousal," "Erection," "Roll Condom On," "Leave Space at Tip (squeeze out air)," "Intercourse," "Orgasm/Ejaculation," "Hold onto Rim," "Withdraw the Penis," "Loss of Erection," "Relaxation," and, finally, an environmental skill, "Throw Condom Out." Note the goose-step courtship suggested to today's robo-lovers: "Talk with Partner," "Decision by Both Partners to Have Sex."

Today's sex educator sees his demystifying task as ensuring not only that kids have the information necessary to avoid disease and pregnancy but also that they have "healthy" attitudes toward sex. A healthy student is one who is "relaxed" and "comfortable" in the presence of the erotic and can speak of sex in the same tones and with the same lack of emotion he might bring to a discussion of carbure-

tors. Giggling kids who appear to suffer from embarrass-
ment or reticence, sure signs of "anti-sex" attitudes or irrational hang-ups, must undergo a program of desensitization.
One exercise I recently heard about at a private school
in Brooklyn attempted such a reeducation, much to the dis-
may of a number of parents: in a fifth-grade class, students
were required to pronounce the words for the genitals at
increasingly louder volume. Children calculating math problems in nearby classrooms were serenaded by their ten-year-
old friends yelling, "Penis! Vagina!!"

The push to rationalize and de-intensify sexual desire is
so total that some educators even try to reprogram their students' fantasy lives. William A. Fisher, a professor of psychology at the University of Ontario, and Deborah M. Roffman, a
sexuality education teacher at the Park School in Brook-
landville, Maryland, suggest one way to steer fantasies into
conformity with the rational ideal. Because teenagers' sexual
fantasies usually don't involve condoms, Fisher and Roffman
propose, why not show them "fantasy walk-throughs" in
stories, videotapes, or plays, where kids like themselves
"successfully perform . . . sex-related preventive behaviors."
"Such imagery," they continue, "should enter teenagers'
memories as fantasy-based scripts for personally practicing
preventive behaviors when or if such behaviors are necessary."

Striking the same chilling, Strangelovian tone of scientific detachment, sex educators object to Hollywood's dream
vision of sex not because coupling is ubiquitous or mechanical but because it is "irresponsible" or "unrealistic," with so
few references to birth control, diseases, or abortion. More
"pro-social messages," according to this line of thinking,
would solve the problem of the hypersexed media.

The examples I've cited are extreme; few children are

treated to classroom exercises precisely like these. Nevertheless such examples expose the inadequacy of the terms of the
culture wars over condom distribution, the Rainbow curriculum, or the promotion of masturbation as a form of safe
sex. What's happening is not as simple as a contest between
enlightened liberals seeking to liberate sexual life from Puritan repressiveness, and life-denying conservatives who wish
to imprison it in a web of moral and religious restrictions.
On closer inspection the sexual liberals turn out to be advancing their own rigid moral strictures. Their Eros lays
down an updated Puritan law: pleasure and self-fulfillment,
yes; passion, no. The question, it begins to seem, isn't
whether a society will codify sexual behavior but how it will
do so. "From authority," Phillip Rieff has written, "there is
no escape"; that authority has simply been transferred from
the church to the clinic.

This medicalization of sex has deposed the irrational
chimera Love and installed reasonable Health as king. Kids
must have "healthy" attitudes; they must make "healthy" decisions. A 1993 *Good Housekeeping*/CBS poll asked teenagers
to give reasons not to have sex. While 85 percent mentioned
fear of AIDS or pregnancy, only 4 percent said "not being in
love." And although the increasing popularity of abstinence
as a value to be taught in the schools may seem like an important shift in the cultural climate, it only perpetuates the
medical-scientific mode of sexual thinking. An article entitled "AIDS Disinformation" in *Seventeen* illustrates the problem: "Seventy-eight percent of women are sexually active by
age 19," it announces. "This is not to say that abstinence isn't
an important option. It is the only way to be 100 percent sure
of not getting HIV through sexual transmission."

Conventional wisdom has it that the hypersexed media
encourage kids to "fool around." But this half-truth begs the

question of where in today's culture a teenager can find any alternative vision, any language for imagining sex as a potentially powerful union. Many parents today mumble something like, "Be careful." Meanwhile their own behavior is corrosive to the idealistic longings of adolescence. In her book *Erotic Wars*, the sociologist Lillian Rubin quotes a promiscuous seventeen-year-old who was twelve when her father left her mother for a younger woman. "I don't want to hear about any of that love stuff," the girl says. "It's garbage, just plain garbage. If a guy wants to make it with a girl, he'll say anything. I just spare them the trouble, that's all. Anyway, what's the big deal?"

Educators second this kind of cynicism when they advise kids only to "talk with partner" or "make healthy, good decisions." On what moral terms should a teen ground this good decision? Here the educators come up empty-handed. A National Guidelines Task Force of sex educators looked into this problem and could offer only platitudes like "Every person has dignity and self-worth," and the priceless "All sexual decisions have effects and consequences." Is it any wonder that kids today, stripped of all spiritualizing ideals and with nothing but dismal "health" to replace them, would shrug and ask, "What's the big deal?"

Love's most powerful enemy may well be America's obsession with individual autonomy. The free, self-contained individual—or "unit," as Cliff puts it in *Singles*—looks with suspicion on emotions that threaten dependence on others, and he celebrates those that glorify his splendid isolation. From this point of view, love might well signal childish weakness. "Clearly, romance can arrive with all its obsession whenever we're feeling incomplete," writes Gloria Steinem in her best-selling 1992 book *Revolution from Within*. "The truth is that finding ourselves brings more excitement and well-being than anything romance has to offer." Steinem's prissy rejection of powerful feeling echoes that of some of her precursors, the nineteenth-century feminists. But it goes a step further. From her perspective, the problem is not merely that love's urgent desire for the other can shade into out-of-control obsession. It is that this obsession sweeps us away from life's central project: finding ourselves.

Finding ourselves is a complex task these days. It means not only developing interests and talents but also "exploring" what we have come to call "our sexuality." While sex is an activity or behavior involving another individual, sexuality is a territory of the self. Its logic insists that we are all "self-contained units." Others must not interfere.

Watch *Oprah* or *Donahue*, pick up any academic treatise on "gender," flip through any sex education curriculum, or read any self-help book and the creed of healthy sexuality will stare you in the face. "Sexuality is much more than 'sex' or 'sexual intercourse,'" explains one sex manual for girls. "It is the entire self as girl or boy or man or woman. . . . Sexuality is a basic part of who we are as a person and affects how we feel about ourselves and all our relationships with others." Though it may affect how we feel about others, it does not necessarily tie us to them, for sexuality is first and foremost a vital arena of self-expression and creativity, a central act in the drama of personal identity. Leah P., married eighteen years and interviewed on a National Public Radio show about sex and marriage, admits she would hesitate to have an affair but insists on her autonomy from any rules or institutions or even relationships: "My sexuality belongs to me. I can take it where I choose to. . . . It doesn't belong to my husband; it doesn't belong to my marriage."

The creed of sexuality demands that the individual "explore" or "develop" her sexuality fully by experimenting with different partners, in different positions, at different times of the day, or in different rooms of the house or office. During the seventies, when the novels of Anaïs Nin and Erica Jong were popular, promiscuity became almost a matter of principle for many women newly liberated from old-fashioned notions of what good girls could and couldn't do. Sexual variety and abundance did not merely promise pleasure; they asserted women's freedom and independence. ("That was the meaning of freedom," thinks Nin's heroine Sabine about a one-night stand in *A Spy in the House of Love*.) And further: to expand one's sexuality was to expand one's very identity.

But if sex is imagined as a meeting of free, autonomous, and creative selves, each engaged in an act of self-exploration, we are left with a problem: the lover—or partner, the current term and one better evoking the situation—is in danger of becoming an object to be used and played with. The connection between partners can then only be imagined as contractual: two free agents voluntarily and conditionally involved in a mutually agreed-upon activity. Some of our best and most disenchanted bureaucratic minds have gotten to work on this, as exemplified by the Fourteen Stages of Condom Use and the famous Antioch College sexual harassment code. "Obtaining consent is an ongoing process in any sexual interaction," the code reads. "Verbal consent should be obtained with each new level of physical or sexual conduct in any given interaction. . . . The request for consent must be specific to each act."

Although it ostensibly prizes freedom and pleasure, the creed of "sexuality" instead produces this sort of leaden, bureaucratic vision of sex. Here, unlike the lover willing to risk opening his heart in hopes of joyful union, the partner becomes a skilled negotiator demanding and accepting conditions for his or her personal pleasure. Hence "sexuality" inevitably restrains the emotional, truly personal connection between lovers, stifling what Stendhal called the "passions which make for deeper joy." Central to an age of personal health and fulfillment, "sexuality" flattens as well as enriches the self-contained, autonomous individual. It giveth and it taketh away.

How entirely fitting, then, that one key battle of the culture wars, highlighted by the firing of Clinton surgeon general Joycelyn Elders, is masturbation. The multiple ironies of teaching the joys of masturbation to teenagers were largely lost in the usual Scopes-trial terms of the brouhaha—either you are anti-sex and believe masturbation makes your palms hairy, or you believe, as one Los Angeles schoolteacher claimed, it is a "way to sexually express yourself without actually having sex." Not least among those ironies is that masturbation does less to enrich sexual life than to advance the project of rational self-sufficiency. No messy emotions here.

Equally ludicrous, but unfortunately dead serious, is the way in which the primacy of the autonomous, self-contained ego freed from the call of passionate love reveals itself in popular culture. "You can find love if you search within yourself," croons Mariah Carey in her hit song "Hero." Accompanied by rich orchestral melodies, the video shows her with the quivering lips and outstretched hands usually associated with deep longing for another. "All I really want is to be happy, but the answer lies in me," sings Mary J. Blige in another big hit. Camille Paglia may have said more than she realized when she joked about her own gigantic ego: "There's Tristan and Iseult, Romeo and Juliet, me and me. It's the love affair of the century!"

At times the sadness of American detachment seeps through the glossiest of advice columns. One example appears in an issue of *YM*, a teen magazine, in an article entitled "The Six Love Wreckers (and How to Avoid Them)." Five of the six "love wreckers," those things girls do that chase boys away, involve loving too much. They include: "You're too demanding. . . . You're too jealous. . . . You push for a commitment." "Some guys get really uncomfortable when you try to box them in," warns one expert. "Plus, you risk coming off as desperate and needy." "Get a life! . . . Doing your own thing will make him appreciate you more," barks another author, under the headline "YOU'RE TOO DEPENDENT." Adult women get similar advice: pronounces a recent *Cosmopolitan* headline, "CLINGY IS OUT!"

Jealousy, possessiveness, and dependence are the stuff of our contemporary morality stories. The man in love is neither a hero nor henpecked as he once was; he is now a stalker or wife-abuser, our contemporary villain. Both the mainstream media and teen magazines frequently carry updated gothic tales like "My Ex Tried to Kill Me" or "When a Lover Turns Evil; He Follows You—Spies on You—Loves You to Death." The O. J. Simpson trial fascinates us in large part because it reminds us of the extremes of these tabooed passions.

In this way popular culture subverts as well as endorses our tidy scientific-therapeutic view of the human condition. Its current fascination with sadomasochism is a perfect example. A 1995 article in *New York* magazine cited many examples, including the fashion photos in *Details* magazine, Gianni Versace's 1992 fashion show with supermodel Cindy Crawford in bondage getup, and plotlines on soap operas, including *One Life to Live* and—one for the teen set—*Beverly Hills 90210*. Though presented as the next stage in a continuing liberation from outdated taboos, the fascination with S&M barely conceals the misery of the robo-lover. Enthusiasts are quick to affirm that S&M sex is "consensual," but with its chains and whips, handcuffs and muzzles, it offers the "partner" one last, desperate chance at surrendering his hardened, encapsulated ego to strong feeling. These sex toys suggest a perverse, high-tech twist on sexual liberation: the man or woman who wants to be dominated and controlled, to give himself up completely to another.

But this interest in S&M reminds us as well that, especially in a rationalized world where a lover's joy pales into pleasure and his tormented longing into co-dependence, irrational fantasy and intense desire will always bubble up. Kids raised in a world without an enriching myth to humanize the Dionysian demons growling and scratching below the surface of civility and to intensify their attachments to another are not a happy sight. For if some teens have reaped the superficial benefits of the new dispensation's relaxation of traditional taboos, all too many suffer from its shallowness.

For girls the results are not just the widely reported epidemic of sexually transmitted diseases and unplanned pregnancies. Also evident to many working with these young women is a sense of vacant joylessness. Fifteen-year-olds with ten or even more "partners"—the sociologist Lillian Rubin interviewed one sixteen-year-old who said she had "forty or fifty"—do not merely fail to find love; ironically, they also fail at the pursuit of pleasure, for they are almost never orgasmic. They promise to become a new generation of embittered women, resentful of men, cynical about love, and ripe for single motherhood.

How could they be otherwise, given the boys they have to contend with? Without any humanizing myth to help quiet the demons, boys have begun to play out the truth of Freud's observation that lust and aggression are deeply intertwined. Reports of young studs "playing rape" in a Yonkers schoolyard during recess, of nine-year-old sexual harassers and fifth-grade rapists and sodomists, have become too common to pass off as simply anomalous. To be sure, boys have always striven to test their manhood through sexual conquest. But the Spur Posse, a gang of teenage boys from Lakewood, California, are just as surely creatures of a crippled emotional culture. The boys held a contest in which they "hooked up"—a tellingly mechanical phrase—with girls as young as ten. (The winner "scored" sixty-six girls.)

Dispiriting as they are, these examples don't totally capture the emotional alienation of this Post-Idealist, Neo-Pragmatic Era of Relationships. In his 1979 book *The Culture of Narcissism*, Christopher Lasch described the recent crop of patients seeking therapy, who, unlike the general run of patients in the past, "tend to cultivate a protective shallowness in emotional relations" and who are "chronically bored, restlessly in search of . . . emotional titillation without involvement and dependence." Therapists today continue to find such emptiness and emotional blankness the most common complaint. In the past, love has had the virtue not only of satisfying our longing for profound connection but of lifting us out of mundane life into enchantment. While it may not have straightened the crooked timber of humanity, it respected and nourished its tortuous imagination. Today more than ever, the sources of that nourishment seem indeed to have dried up.

[1995]

9

J. Crew U.

Most parents setting out to choose a college for their son or daughter are probably prepared for a campus vastly changed from their own day. Coed dorms, date-rape hot lines, diversity sensitivity groups, and most notably multiculturalism will surprise no one half-conscious during the past decade. Somewhat obscured behind the contentiousness of these changes, though, is a related, equally momentous shift: the complete disappearance of a fixed, coherent curriculum and with it any shared notion of the well-educated man or woman. All that once ordered higher education—requirements for majors, the traditional disciplines, the core curriculum—is vanishing into the chaos of postmodernism. "The closer one looks, the more arguments about 'the' university curriculum splinter into a zillion courses," writes Russell Jacoby in *Dogmatic Wisdom*. "There is no curriculum." It is as if Americans have stood around arguing about who was going to drive while a thief sped off with the car.

Critics of the academy from both the left and the right have rightly bemoaned the current curriculum—if that is even the word for it—as fragmentated and incoherent. Yet out of the smoldering curricular ruins has inevitably arisen an organizing force of sorts. That force is simply the individual student or, as we used to say in my house during the especially trying days of early parenthood, Himself: his whims, his desires, his inchoate (and, to be honest, frequently flawed) judgment, or—in the portentous words of the glossy PR materials that now chase any student with a respectable showing on his PSAT—his "individual educational needs." The admissions director from Wesleyan proudly summed it up at a college-night talk at my son's high school. An applicant asked what the director thought the university's biggest problem was. "Our biggest problem is also our greatest strength," he replied enthusiastically. "Students are on their own. They have to figure things out for themselves. We're not going to tell them what they should study or what they should be."

Many parents, living with kids whose idea of what they want to study might be more easily satisfied at a downtown dance club than a campus lecture hall, might wonder how institutions devoted to the education of late adolescents can demonstrate so little grasp of their nature. Indeed, the college advertisements depict a student as unreal, as idealized as the smiling, handsomely outfitted models in the J. Crew catalogs these documents so resemble. And the brochures also hint at the deeper weakness at the heart of the do-your-own-thing curriculum. For the academy is spawning a perilous myth for its still-developing charges: that they can, in all their ripe perfection, step outside society and each create his own one-man culture.

The college brochures yield plenty of examples of how the academy has tried to transform the shattering of the curriculum into a boon for students. These materials are laden with what a postmodernist given to self-reflection might term a discourse of contemporary American desire. *Flexibility, open-*

ness, independence, freedom: the language of the promotional literature is so uniform it seems that every admissions office from Occidental to Harvard has uploaded the same public relations software program. Grinnell, enthuses one student in the Iowa school's recruitment material, a fine example of the genre, "offers something most schools don't. It gives you the chance to be in charge of your education." "Students are independent," proclaims the director of admissions. "Free from core requirements, they design programs that fulfill their own educational needs."

Nor do the elite schools have any higher vision to offer of the purpose of college education. "We have no requirements," announced the admissions director from Amherst during a college-night sales pitch. Pause for the good news to sink in: "No requirements." (She was not being 100 percent honest. Like many schools, Amherst requires an interdisciplinary team-taught freshman seminar—about which more later.) Admissions people at Smith, Vassar, Wellesley, and Brown, the school that under the prodding of Ira Magaziner first gave us the libertarian curriculum, could claim much the same. To put it in plain English, college students can do just about whatever they want. No wonder Camille Paglia compares college today to summer camp.

The sheer proliferation of courses, a kind of sorcerer's apprentice approach to the curriculum, amplifies the illusion of undergraduate freedom. The University of Pennsylvania boasts a mind-numbing 2,000 courses but is easily—in fact literally—outclassed by nearby Rutgers, with 4,000. On a smaller scale this kind of variety was always a selling point in larger universities. But today smaller schools also strive for the megacurriculum. Amherst now boasts 600 offerings—but will have to try harder if it wants to compete with Washington and Lee. "In 1985, the *Washington Post* noted that 'Washington and Lee's 700-course catalogue is the envy of many larger institutions,'" proudly states the brochure for this Virginia school. "In the decade since that quote appeared, the curriculum has grown to include more than 900 different courses." Following this progression, the next decade might find this small liberal arts college (enrollment: 1,620) with more courses than students.

True, most brochures refer to something called "distribution requirements": students must take two or three courses from several general categories, most commonly the humanities, the social sciences, and the natural sciences and math. But the hundreds or thousands of choices available to students stretch the distribution requirement to the borders of triviality—and beyond. The natural sciences and math requirement, for instance, can be satisfied at many schools by courses like "Ethno-Biology" or "Math for the Artist." Furthermore, according to a study by the National Association of Scholars titled "The Dissolution of General Education: 1914–1993," introductory courses are fast disappearing. A typical undergrad can easily receive his first and only taste of sociology, say, by studying not Durkheim and Weber but battered women in India.

In other words, students spend their four years browsing the Shopping Mall University, to borrow a phrase from a book, *The Shopping Mall High School*, that describes the same trend in secondary schools. There they are free to try on whatever looks enticing—Shakespearean plays or mulatto novels, thirties America or Ming Dynasty China. Michael Moffatt, an anthropologist who lived among Rutgers students in the 1980s and published his findings in a book titled *Coming of Age in New Jersey*, found that Rutgers's distribution formula, which requires a major, a minor, and a mini, one from each of three categories—Humanities/

Languages, Social Studies, and Science/Mathematics—doesn't preclude a rigorous curriculum in, say, English, history, and physics. But it also allows a student to choose a major in dance, a minor in sports studies, and a mini in meteorology.

Though the groaning board of curricular offerings promises satisfaction for every taste and desire, the colleges have not fully escaped one tiresome demand on their students: the major. And where there are majors, there must be requirements, right? But potential applicants need not worry; this wrinkle won't constrain their individuality. Most schools, no matter how small, boast majors in the mid to high double digits; the State University of New York at Albany, which calls itself "A Place for Individuals," is on the low side with fifty-three majors compared, say, with Rutgers with one hundred. But beyond that, colleges also invite students to create their own majors. The term *major* is now sometimes qualified into "major" in roguish postmodern fashion, a message to seventeen-year-old applicants that they should remember that the traditional disciplines are social inventions of dubious value and, as such, a potential barrier to personal expression.

It's rare to find a school that doesn't now promise "Our Unique Interdisciplinary Program" or, as Carnegie Mellon more grandly calls it, "The Freedom of Interdisciplinary Programs." "Our unique Teaching Program of the University Professors," announces the Boston University admissions department, "allows interested students to design their own courses of study, often bridging the gap left by traditional majors." At the University of Pennsylvania they just come out and say it: "Students are able to combine their interests, even if they are seemingly unrelated." "Our curriculum is uniquely open," proclaims the classy brochure from Eugene

J. Crew U.

Lang College of the New School, its dusty blue, pink, and purple lettering on a sleek black background befitting its downtown image. "Students design their own programs."

With all this uniqueness it may be surprising to find that eight pounds of college brochures (literally—I weighed them) from schools as diverse as Albright and Amherst still tend to sketch, much like the fashion catalogs that appear so to have influenced them, a remarkably similar picture of the model undergrad in their student blurbs. It's an appealing picture, to be sure. He is intensely curious, eager to "explore" the universe of the megacurriculum. At the same time, this ideal student is so full of passion and commitment as barely to be contained within ivy walls. He is both cosmopolitan and socially committed, equally at home in soup kitchens and Paris cafés, Indian reservations and Japanese teahouses. Above all else, he is "creative," a word that is so much a cliché among American educationalists these days that it has truly earned deconstructive quotation marks. Released from the chains of required courses and traditional disciplines, the model student soars into the unknown, discovering "new perspectives." This student is a new Renaissance man or woman gliding gracefully between the sciences and the arts, making what an issue of the *Brandeis Review* calls "Curricular Connections: Tools for Genius." Every student may be an island—but what a magnificent island, what a fertile island!

These model kids sound prodigiously impressive. Franklin and Marshall showcases one student who traveled to Jerusalem to study the theological manuscripts of Sir Isaac Newton and another who went to Tanzania to make a documentary film on homeless children. Yet these blurbs sometimes have the breathless romantic quality of a slush-pile movie script—which should give pause to those who look back on their college years with a clear eye. Take this description by a class of '95 Connecticut College graduate, a narrative worth quoting at length: "In the classroom, my learning crossed disciplines. . . . I designed two independent studies . . . and as Georgia O'Keeffe once said, 'began to voice things in my head that are not like what anyone has taught me.' A deep personal interest in American Indian issues and economic development surfaced this year through an independent study in the economics department and an internship at the nearby Mashantucket Pequot reservation. In September I will go seek my fortunes in Missoula, Montana. There, I hope to work on the Flathead Indian Reservation on economic development, learn to play cello, collect tacky magnets, and drive a truck. Who knows? Maybe I'll take up fly fishing and marry a cowboy."

The dreaminess of this scenario is no accident. For the libertarian curriculum and the discourse of freedom and independence that have nurtured this Emma Bovary of the nineties are mythological to the core. The myth of the college brochure begins with an illusory student: not just independent but self-motivated, passionate, self-aware, well informed. Consider instead the reality of the college student just graduated from an American public school. Now he must decide how best to meet his educational needs. Surveys suggest he knows little about, among many other things, American history. Does he ponder his ignorance in this area and sign up for an American history course? Of course not. The libertarian curriculum neglects the obvious: the student doesn't know what he doesn't know. Further, he doesn't know what he needs to know to be a well-informed member of society. That's why someone invented required courses.

If, as is undoubtedly the case, some students are guided by "deep personal interests" in choosing their courses—by the passion and drive admissions directors like to celebrate—most are moved by more mundane concerns. Michael Moffatt, the anthropologist who studied Rutgers students, found that they chose their courses not out of passion or even curiosity but after "intricate calculations of and trade-offs of necessity, interest, convenience, availability, and difficulty." In the glossy brochures, students may seek new challenges; in the dorms, they cross off demanding professors and no-time-for-breakfast 9 a.m. classes. Denied any clear vision of the purpose of a general education, students, Moffatt found, divided Rutgers's megacurriculum "in a very simple way. There were useful subjects, subjects that presumably led to good careers, and there were useless ones," namely the humanities.

This coarse practicality suggests that the socially concerned, activist student may be another ivory-tower fantasy character rather than a flesh-and-blood undergrad. A longitudinal study by the UCLA Higher Education Research Institute begun in 1985 found that though political commitment and activism among students increases somewhat during their years on campus, the numbers are unimpressive, and such commitment as there is doesn't last. Twenty-four percent of seniors cited a "desire to influence politics" as an important goal, up from 19 percent when these same students were freshmen. A mere four years after graduation, the number had plummeted to 14 percent.

Similarly, 27 percent of freshmen called "participating in community action programs" an important goal. This number had increased to 35 percent by the time they were seniors but had dipped to 23 percent four years later. Evidently the modest number of students influenced by campus politics remember their lessons about social activism about as long as they remember Anthropology 101.

This may be because in the real world, unlike the J. Crew-land of the college brochure, kids tend to follow what their elders do rather than what they say. Professors may mouth elevated precepts about social justice, but they also serve as a good model for the crude vocationalism that Moffatt and many others have noted. Students learn it in the many courses designed by professors more interested in developing a paper for the next conference in San Diego than in educating the next generation. The boutique freshman seminar, one of the few required courses left in many schools, reads like a card catalog of recently completed dissertations and books and articles in progress, with salable, career-boosting titles like "Sisterhood in Contemporary Literature" or "Animal Rights and Wrongs."

But students' careerism and disengagement can only very partially be blamed on individual professors who are, after all, laboring in a system that values success on the conference circuit over good teaching in the classroom. The truth is, these qualities are inevitable consequences of the solipsism inherent in the shopping-mall curriculum. Hundreds, if not thousands, of courses train today's students in the mystique of specialization, which renders archaic the entire notion of a shared world of knowledge. Over four years, each student may well have enrolled in more than thirty classes entirely different not just from those of his roommate but from those of his entire dormitory. The freshman seminar can have as many listings as a smalltown phone book—seventy-five different possibilities at the University of Pennsylvania, for instance. Notes a student from Grinnell: "I always find it mildly ironic that the one course everyone at this college is 'forced' to take turns out to be the one thing that presents students with the most diverse individual set of experiences."

Such an approach, with its glorification of unencumbered autonomy and individual choice, provides no foundation for social solidarity and active citizenship. For one thing, students in all likelihood will graduate without any real grasp of their nation's history or its intellectual or cultural traditions, now lumped with the "useless" humanities. The sovereign, solitary undergraduate learns that he wanders in a universe of his own making rather than in what the authors of *Habits of the Heart* call a "community of memory." Having undermined any means of evoking in their students a sense of a shared past or a shared destiny, professors instead attempt to instill feelings of *élite oblige*, for the homeless, say, or for AIDS patients. Sure, concern for the downtrodden is an essential part of our civic obligation; but the amnesiac, however compassionate, does not a citizen make.

And here is the underlying irony of the libertarian mega-curriculum. Contemporary academics like to speak of "decentering" or "subverting" the individual. The autonomous self is a fiction, they aver; the "individual" is but a passive medium through which the voices of gender, class, race, and ethnicity recite their ideologies. Yet, oddly enough, those same professors have promoted an educational system that exalts the autonomous individual—the green inchoate, adolescent individual at that. In demolishing the notion of a relatively stable body of knowledge, a traditional set of disciplines to which developing thinkers must apprentice themselves, they have invited their students, though half formed and ill educated, to indulge in a fantasy of their own extravagant powers. Here is how the dean of admissions describes the academic experience at his reputable liberal arts college: "At Franklin and Marshall, we don't hand you a packaged education. We help you identify the materials for your own educational endeavors; you then develop skills with which you can mold those materials most creatively and effectively." The "packaged education," which I take to mean the vanquished core curriculum of literature, philosophy, and the arts and sciences, is translated into "materials" on which the young can exercise their "creativity," as if they were giants standing on the shoulders of dwarfs. The legacy of the past has no real power over our young talents: it is merely a set of "tools for genius."

In this sense one could reasonably argue that the current curriculum is more anticultural than multicultural. While some professors may rail about the hold of race and gender on identity, the structure of the education they have invented gives a very different message: that the past has no weight. It is not a living presence in which each of us is inextricably embedded. Rather, it is bunk, a barrier to self-fulfillment. This shrugging attitude toward the past is epitomized by both the relentless presentism and topicality of today's college courses and the blurring of the traditional disciplines. Yet by promoting a skeptical attitude toward the very idea of an independently existing, historically continuous reality, the postmodernists seduce the next generation into imagining themselves as having stepped outside cultural constraint, precisely the opposite of what they profess to believe possible.

If these ideas sound vaguely familiar, that's because they hark back to an American tradition embodied most strongly by Emerson and Thoreau. "Why should we grope among the dry bones of the past?" asked Emerson. "Why should not we also enjoy an original relation to the universe?" In short, the ideal of the individual released from history and social identity, and creating his own reality, has a fine American pedigree. This ideal may be highly problematic as the foundation for an educational philosophy and, for that matter, as the basis for a coherent culture. Still, don't count on Emerson's ideas becoming the subject of intelligent debate. Most students, ignorant of the past he epitomizes, look as if they will simply be condemned to repeat it. So much for the freedom and creativity of the next generation.

[1996]

10

Ecstatic Capitalism's
Brave New Work Ethic

In 1969 I dropped out of college and drove to San Francisco with my boyfriend in a wheezy Ford Falcon to join thousands of other bell-bottomed postadolescents hanging out in Golden Gate Park and the streets around Haight-Ashbury. It was easy enough to tell what these people stood for but impossible to know how they made a living. Rejecting what they viewed as the soul-killing demands of bourgeois life, they were there not to work but to play, to seek what Hillary Clinton called, in her now-famous Wellesley graduation speech that year, "more immediate, ecstatic, penetrating modes of living." My boyfriend and I were no different. We shared the same career aspirations—which is to say, none. To put food in our mouths, he would take a temporary teaching job, though he thought that driving a cab sounded cool; maybe I would get a job in a store. We weren't worried: rents were cheap, we were young, we had a safety net in the form of suburban parents and heads swimming with the utopian dreams of our generation.

To go to San Francisco in the 1990s was to be struck with a weird kind of *déjà vu*: hordes of the idealistic young, acutely conscious of being part of a revolution that their elders only dimly understand, still dominated the city. But there the resemblance with the youthquake of thirty years ago ends. These Banana Republic–clad revolutionaries work like immigrants. They talk of nothing but work; they spend ten, twelve, fourteen or even more hours per day at work; they dream of work.

Pragmatists would explain their zeal by skyrocketing rent and real estate costs; cynics would say the crass materialism long threatening to overwhelm the American spirit has finally triumphed. Although both of these explanations have some truth, neither tells the whole story. For to hear them talk, these young men and women also love the risk, the intensity, the speed, the camaraderie, even what they sometimes call the "soulfulness" of work in the new economy. In the late sixties our idea of the wind through our hair was *Zen and the Art of Motorcycle Maintenance*; theirs is *Fast Company* ("More than a Magazine—It's a Movement!"). Our notion of scenery was Big Sur and the hills of fragrant eucalyptus; theirs is the office park. Our idea of a drug was hashish; theirs is Café Grande. In short, if our religion was Peace and Love, theirs is Ecstatic Capitalism.

Make no mistake though: ecstatic capitalism is no mere local or generational phenomenon. Yes, its Rome is San Francisco and Silicon Valley, and its prophets are largely under thirty, but its followers are everywhere and include everyone from recent entrants to the AARP to college kids to (amazingly) preschoolers. True, not everyone is as fervent as the young crusaders of the high-tech sector. But it's pretty clear that while Americans are deeply divided over many of the cultural values that they once took for granted, just about everyone embraces a high-energy, high-spirited new work ethic.

Increasingly we view work not just as a way to pay the rent and the orthodontist but as an end in itself. We expect work to offer excitement or "serious fun," as the editors of *Fast Company* put it; we seek in work both individual meaning and community in a way that defies not just the counter-cultural expectations of thirty years ago but much of our philosophical and intellectual tradition. And yet this hardly means that utopia is on its way. The costs of this unexpected transformation in the national psyche may be subtle, but they are a bit disquieting nonetheless.

If you want to see ecstatic capitalism in its purest form, visit a place like Sparks.com, a young start-up company selling greeting cards over the Internet. Sparks occupies a cavernous warehouse in San Francisco's India Basin, far from the city's sophisticated cafés and shops, beyond even the train tracks at its edges. Inside the warehouse you find a cross between a college dorm and a campaign war room. Each employee sits at a plank of wood on two sawhorses, individually decorated with company-supplied paint. An amateurish mural showing the joyous smiles of pleasure caused by a Sparks greeting card takes up one wall. The "conference room's" shag rug and bright yellow and orange beanbag chairs, along with the warehouse's fooball table and basketball court, further confound all conventional notions of "workplace."

As the ponytailed chief technical officer skateboards through the aisles in his workshirt and sneakers, young engineers in T-shirts consult with one another, ignoring the blaring rock music and the occasional dog sniffing at their feet. They also have to shout over the sound of the hammers and drills of workmen who, following the request of Sparks's employees, are installing a giant sliding board and fire pole between the new loft and ground floor. On Friday afternoons the group has barbecues; in October, pumpkin-decorating parties. A "corporate massage therapist" visits regularly.

This playful exuberance coexists with a zealous work ethic. Allison Behr, the 29-year-old public relations director who is showing me around, tells me that she works eleven hours a day, except during the weeks near the Christmas rush, when everyone at Sparks burns the midnight oil. In her world this is no oddity—area legend has it that when a 24-year-old Netscape programmer told a survey company that he worked between 110 and 120 hours per week, the researcher objected that his computerized questionnaire wouldn't accept a number that big. Allison has no complaints. Yes, she has to do her grocery shopping at 10 p.m., but "it's a good time to shop, because it isn't crowded." Beyond that, Allison says, "I don't do a lot of errands because I'm having too much fun with my co-workers." The spirit of camaraderie is ever present: "You rarely see people here doing anything alone," she reports. Like many ecstatic capitalists, Allison is partial to the word "soul": "It's important to us that we do things that are soulful." "Our hearts and souls and guts go into this." "Sparks is a company with soul."

Sparks perfectly captures ecstatic capitalism's major themes—the long hours, the blurring between work and play, the youthful energy and intensity, the sense of both individual meaning and recovered community in a fragmented world. Observers of the dot.com scene have been noting all this for close to a decade, but now this redefined work ethic is colonizing adjacent sectors of the new economy. Knowledge workers in all fields are working like mad, as are young singles in general: the Families and Work Institute found that 73 percent of today's twenty-five- to thirty-two-year-olds work more than forty hours per week, compared with 55 percent in 1977. And Arlie Hochschild reports in *The Time*

Bind that when a Fortune 500 company offered workers ways to cut back their hours, the employees—and especially women with children—rarely took advantage of them.

Work now spreads out of the cubicle and oozes into just about every corner of our lives. *Fast Company* profiled Steelcase, a giant office-furniture manufacturer in Grand Rapids, Michigan, seemingly light years away from the 24/7 digerati outfits in Redwood City or Austin. Yet Steelcase shows dramatically how completely the new-economy ethos is being grafted onto old-economy businesses. Christine Albertini, vice president and general manager, describes habits that make an official category like "working hours" seem quaint: "I work in the car, home, office, airplane, hotel room, on the street corner," she says. "I work at volleyball practice, hockey games, gymnastics," seconds her marketing communications manager.

In this spirit, Steelcase is expanding the entire notion of office furniture. "Their job," reports *Fast Company*, "is to figure out how to furnish the whole world so you can work in it, effortlessly, seamlessly, continuously"—something that any recent traveler can attest has already happened. Airports are outfitted with computer connections, fax machines, and workstations; planes and trains are simply cubicles that happen to be speeding through cumulus clouds and fields of green while you make business calls and work your spreadsheet. And when you arrive at even the most alluring destination, you simply settle into another office away from the office. Marriott hotels have installed more than twenty thousand "Rooms That Work," with special desks, phone jacks, ergonomic chairs, and around-the-room Internet access. Hyatt hotels now offer "Plug and Play" Internet access to their customers.

So why aren't American workers rising up and storming

the CEO offices at the prospect of what Netscape program-
mers once dubbed "all work, all the time"? A thirty-year-old
quoted in *Fortune* explains: "Work is not work. It's a hobby
you happen to get paid for." Knowledge work satisfies
human longings in a way that factory or traditional corporate work rarely could. It requires thinking and creativity.
New management theories stressing the autonomy of individual employees have softened the coercive, hierarchical
nature of work. Many Americans now expect their job to feel
as if it were an emanation of their own desires and on their
own time.

In fact, our jobs define our identity. In France and En-
gland it's bad form to ask, "What do you do?" Such a rule
would leave Americans speechless. In the United States you
are what you do. Management guru Tom Peters has even
written a book entitled *The Brand Called You*, in which he
urges workers to imagine themselves as the company and
the product. "You are CEO of Me Inc.," he writes. "[T]o grow
your brand you've got to come to terms with power—your
own."

This Nietzsche-in-the-cubicle philosophy has a spiritual
side that appears to be especially appealing to Gen-Xers.
"Our generation has a spiritual void in the space previously
filled by religion or patriotism," the young editor of
Silicon Alley Reporter writes. "[L]ifelong learning and self-
development will become our generation's new religion."

It's in the more innovative sectors of the new economy
that work has taken on the most existential quality, the
naked self realizing itself in a test against the elements. Tom
Ashbrook's memoir *The Leap*, a title combining athleticism
and faith, is a good example of what we might call X-treme
work. Nearing forty, a happily married suburban father of
three, a writer and editor at the *Boston Globe*, Ashbrook nev-

ertheless felt himself "a hungry soul." But if midlife crises led men of a previous generation to love affairs or sports cars, Ashbrook looked to the new economy to awaken his deadened spirit: he decided to start an Internet company.

Like an athlete, he gives up coffee in order to seek "a natural high." He wants his adventure to take him "from security to risk. From the known to the unknown. From well-grazed limits to open vistas"—and in a way it does, when, after superhuman hours, salaryless months, and reckless borrowing, he nearly lands in bankruptcy and divorce court. But by the end of his story, this reporter, who had once traveled to third world countries with his social conscience on his sleeve, now sheds the tears of a champion in the new-economy marathon, a wholehearted convert to ecstatic capitalism, when his dot.com business finally takes off.

Though few Americans will probably ever experience the thrill of X-treme work, ecstatic capitalism's blurring of work and play affects all areas of the economy. Younger companies sponsor capture-the-flag games or afternoons of paintball tournaments. Other firms boast putting greens, horseshoe pits, and game rooms with pinball machines and Ping-Pong tables. People walk through the hallways in socks or bare feet; they decorate their cubicles with their favorite toys. Work is so fun and cool that it has even become a fashion statement. A recent Banana Republic ad campaign set in an office shows a svelte young woman holding a phone to her ear with her head thrown back, laughing hilariously, as a hand holds out another phone toward her. What's so funny? The only text is the same as the other ads in this campaign: the word "Work."

According to most of our philosophy and religion, not to mention our historical experience, none of this makes much sense. Work and play, labor and pleasure, were supposed to be opposites. In the Bible, paradise offers leisure and ease; out of Eden, man must earn his bread by the sweat of his brow. Work was supposed to be all dutiful superego—Freud believed that it rested on a renunciation of erotic instinct; leisure was id, freedom, festivals. Anyone who could manage to avoid work would; that's why we talk—or used to talk—of the idle rich.

Nineteenth-century utopian novels like Edward Bellamy's *Looking Backward* and William Dean Howells's *A Traveler from Altruria* assumed that progress would inevitably lead to leisure, with time for hobbies, civic engagement, family, and neighborly sociability. Benjamin Hunnicutt, author of *Work Without End* and professor of leisure studies (!) at the University of Iowa, notes that the American labor movement's very first pamphlet was an early-nineteenth-century call for reducing daily work hours from twelve to ten and eventually to eight or even six. Even when work moved increasingly from the factory to the corporate office, social critics continued to contrast the world of work, which forced men in Grey Flannel Suits into a mold of dehumanizing conformity, with the world of home and leisure, where they could be themselves. As Peter and Brigitte Berger wrote in *The Homeless Mind*: "The private sphere has served as a kind of balancing mechanism providing meanings and meaningful activities for the discontents brought about by the large structures of modern society."

Sixties gurus, including Charles Reich in *The Greening of America*, echoed the nineteenth-century utopians and predicted the coming of a new day when technology-driven abundance would expand the opportunities for self-expression in leisure and private life. Less sanguine, Daniel Bell warned in *The Cultural Contradictions of Capitalism* in 1976 that, once released, hedonism would undermine and even vanquish the work ethic, something that seemed already coming to pass around Haight-Ashbury in 1969.

But even as Bell was writing, the opposition between work and leisurely individual expression, public and private, was already easing: as David Brooks put it in a subchapter heading in his 2000 *Bobos in Paradise*, "The Cultural Contradictions of Capitalism—Resolved!" Feminists began the process. In her 1963 *Feminine Mystique*, Betty Friedan announced that it was the home that was the prison, while the public sphere promised self-expression and liberation. Though Christopher Lasch argued that Friedan's book was less a call for women to go to the office than for "commitment" to volunteer work, say, or to other sorts of civic participation, later feminists balked. The only route to women's liberation, they argued, was paid work.

The much discussed discontents of the Organization Man didn't worry them. They saw work as offering women freedom from the restrictive, stereotypical roles of wife and mother. Public ambition—work life in particular—increasingly came to seem the way one could express the real self. Throughout her recent book, *Flux*, Peggy Orenstein dramatizes how contemporary feminists take these ideas for granted. Career, she says, "requires the assertion of self," whereas relationships "repress . . . [one's] essential self." As for motherhood: "Your whole identity as a person gets swallowed up in [a baby]," she fears. These words mark an amazing transformation: work is now the arena where the true self can blossom; private life and the leisure it offers threaten to make us boring and inauthentic.

Today's workamaniacs wholly subscribe to the feminists' reversal of the traditional distinction between public and private. Work, in the words of *Fast Company*, "is personal." Accordingly, the ecstatic workplace is inviting, even home-like: it's "not just a place to work," says the on-line magazine *Ecompany*. "It's a place to live." Many companies now provide "nap tents" or "spent tents," with sleeping bags, pillows, alarm clocks, soothing music, and a supply of new toothbrushes. One New York media company has a book-lined "womb room," with comfortable chairs and hardwood floors. A growing number of employers are hiring "convenience coordinators" or concierges who locate specialty gifts, find a housekeeper, plan a Hawaiian vacation or a child's birthday party. In this spirit some companies now call their human resources departments "People Offices," headed by "Chief People Officers," or CPOs. Some workers have substituted their co-workers for the family they no longer have time for: "I miss everyone when I go on vacation"; "TCS is my family," write two employees of The Container Store, number one on *Fortune*'s list of Best Companies to Work For.

Ecstatic work, then, is not only personal—it's communal. This explains why, despite the predicted rise in "free agency," self-employment actually fell between 1994 and 1999, for the first five-year period since the 1960s. Instead of starting up in their own garages, millions of workers have joined existing businesses, most of them large companies with at least a thousand employees. Why? According to the *New York Times*, "these workers say that a traditional office—despite all its problems—has become one of the last places to find a community."

It helps that companies provide all sorts of services that you used to have to drive to town to find: auto repair, dry cleaners, even "wellness centers," where you can have your blood pressure or cholesterol monitored. The SAS Institute in Cary, North Carolina, offers breast-cancer and single-parent support groups as well as Bible study groups. Cutting-edge corporate design firms have set out to evoke the spirit of community by turning the workplace into a Disneyland office-village, made all the more appealing because it has none of the garbage, traffic, or (presumably) idiots you have to contend with in the real thing. The cubicles and offices at the TBWA/Chiat/Day advertising firm in Los Angeles, which one employee says is "like a big playground," line the "streets" feeding onto a "Main Street," which leads to a tree-lined "Central Park," where employees can sit in café chairs and sip coffee while they work. A company called Netp@rk is planning New Age office parks where you could arrive in the morning, drop your baby off at the day-care center, your mother at the elder-care center, and Fido at the kennel. At your desk you could log on to your computer and check on them at any time. You could also take a break and go for a swim in the company pool, jog on the company track, or hike along the company nature trail. When it comes to pass, Netp@rk will be the objective correlative of ecstatic capitalism, the total workplace that satisfies all your needs.

Ecstatic capitalism has bored so deeply into the national psyche that it has even changed how Americans think of childhood. For just as Mom goes off to work—as did 59 percent of women with babies under one year old in 1998, versus 31 percent in 1976—and Dad goes off to work, so baby . . . well, goes to work. While a generation ago experts saw infancy as a time to develop healthy emotional attachments, contemporary parenting magazines and advice books are obsessed with "learning" or what *Newsweek* has called "building baby's brain," presumably for the demands of knowledge work. According to the Toy Manufacturer's Association of America, while sales of traditional infant and toddler toys have remained flat, technology-driven "learning toys," a category that didn't even exist twenty-five years ago, have taken off. Growing in popularity are software programs, like "Jumpstart Baby," that come with a BabyBall—an oversize, drool-proof computer mouse for infants as young as nine months.

After a lesson-packed infancy, the new-economy baby must begin school as early as possible. One New York City foreign-language program starts babies at six months—before they can talk—and public pressure is mounting for universal preschool for three- and four-year-olds. For today's five-year-old, a full day's work is mandatory: "No Time for Napping in Today's Kindergarten," proclaims a recent *New York Times* article. One Seneca Falls mother of seven was startled when her youngest child, during her first week of kindergarten, studied the parts of bees and was asked to keep a journal. She shook her head in amazement at the change from when her older children tearfully left the nest: "Never mind the mother-child separation; it's get to work!"

The new-economy grade-schooler also has no time for childish nonsense. Many districts have jettisoned gym and even recess. During the summer, kids go to computer camps, language immersion schools, and enrichment programs: for, as parenting magazines warn, LEARNING TAKES NO VACATION. Tutoring centers like Sylvan Centers and Score! have become the after-school and summer homes of a growing number of children on the move. (Score!'s CEO, Jeff Colon, has said that his centers are most popular in the Bay Area, where parents are especially tuned in to the demands of the knowledge economy.) Chicago parents can send their youngsters to the Children's Health and Executive Club, with its miniature stair-climbing machine equipped with Magna Doodles for developing eye-hand coordination (to improve a child's reading skills) and body balance (to improve math skills). The company's founder, who added a 7 a.m. breakfast club, promises to develop a "positive child, motivated to excel."

LIBERATION'S CHILDREN

Most striking are the children who have absorbed the lessons of ecstatic capitalism so precociously that they are leaping past such jejune concerns as baseball and homework—and even school itself—to go straight to work. James U. McNeal, the country's leading researcher on children's consumption habits, says that younger and younger kids are making money mowing the lawn, cooking meals, and baby-sitting, so that by 1997 the typical ten-year-old had close to fourteen dollars in weekly spending money, a 75 percent increase over 1991. The *Dallas Morning News* reports a new breed of child entrepreneur, outfitted with business cards, credit cards, beepers, cell phones, and Palm Vs. Some of these young workers are in the old-fashioned lawn-cutting business, but others have spied a market for video-rental delivery and the like; still others, according to the article, are just "networking." They may well have gotten advice from one of an emerging genre of child business books like *Making Cents: Every Kid's Guide to Money* or *Girls and Young Women Entrepreneurs: True Stories About Starting and Running a Business.*

As for adolescents, nearly 18 percent of older teens are working at least twenty hours per week during the school year, according to the National Longitudinal Study of Adolescent Health, a record number that far exceeds teen working hours in other industrialized countries. Most working teens serve pizza and Big Macs, but more and more troubleshoot computers for $50 an hour, money they then use to trade stocks over the Internet. Some of these techies simply forgo college, a trend that may partly explain the decline in high school grads attending college—from 67 percent in 1997 to 63 percent in 1999. The *New York Times* reported that one such high school senior, earning "between $30,000 and $40,000" a year, had just made an offer on a $136,000 house near his hometown of Tiffin, Ohio. Says a Missouri twenty-year-old who went straight to Silicon Valley after high school graduation and who now makes $50,000 a year and boasts of his $350,000 in stock options: "In this field, if you go to college, you're outdated."

Only the most curmudgeonly technophobe could fail to be impressed by the staggering amount of motivation, verve, and youthful energy that the new economy has unleashed. But you could forgive him for reminding us of the costs of its novel religion, for all its advantages. To begin with the most obvious, even if work today more nearly approximates play than it has in the past, it can never achieve the nonutilitarian randomness, the release, the freely chosen quality of play. Inevitably, 24/7 work ties us in knots; check out the number of *Fast Company* articles on stress along with desktop "calming pools" for sale at department stores and the demand for corporate massage therapists.

Stress among workamaniac teens has become a theme in newspaper living sections. One *New York Times*–CBS News survey found that affluent teenagers were more likely than their less wealthy peers to complain of stress and, amazingly, to believe that their lives are harder than their parents' lives had been. A senior from St. Louis interviewed in *Time* gets up at 5 a.m. for track practice after only six hours of sleep. After a full day of school and play rehearsal, she comes home to three hours of homework. She doesn't date—"I just don't have the time"—and like many kids her age keeps a day planner to try to pencil in an hour here or there to see friends. More disturbing is how, as child development becomes the equivalent of career training, and as work success becomes the one agreed-upon parental goal, this pressure is passed on to young children: "Failing at Four" is the pathetic title of one *New York* magazine article. A few years ago, the hour a week my daughter's fifth-grade class gives over to personal issues began not with warnings about drugs or hormonal changes but advice about how to handle stress.

Like most religions, ecstatic capitalism can be a totalizing system, and it cannot make sense of those things that do not fit its orthodoxy, especially domestic life. True, many companies now offer flextime and at-home Internet connections whose avowed purpose is to ease work-family tensions. But let's face it: the ultimate goal of these perks is to lower employee stress levels only so they can work more efficiently. In a profile in the *New Yorker*, Larissa MacFarquhar quotes Michael Saylor, head of MicroStrategy, as he pitches his company to a group of new recruits. " 'Who are we competing with in order to capture your hearts and minds? . . . Other software companies? Other employers? What else?' He paused. No one could think of any other answer. 'Anything else you could do with your time,' came Saylor's response. 'You could stay at home, raise the kids, go to college, write the Great American Novel, or slit your wrists and end it all. . . . My job is to make sure that I'm providing you with a combination of economic, psychic, and emotional benefits that makes working for MicroStrategy better than anything else you can do.' " In other words, the company does not simply offer a womb room; it wants to be your mother—and, for that matter, your wife.

But by playing wife and mother, ecstatic capitalism inevitably devalues those intimate relationships. When companies take care of preparing meals or buying a birthday gift for a spouse, they drain those activities of personal meaning. They cast cooking dinner for the family or planning a birthday party as nuisances, of no more significance or pleasure than a trip to Midas Muffler. Sparks.com perfectly exemplifies this tendency. Founder Felicia Lindau, driving home from work one day in 1997, remembered that the next day was her mother's birthday. It was too late to buy a card, but not too late to turn her carelessness into a business idea: a company where you can buy greeting cards 24/7. Better yet, a company that could "manage all of your relationships," as Sparks's website puts it: give them a list of cards you want sent for the next year, and they'll take care of each of them on the proper day. You don't have to give your mother's birthday another thought!

As the total workplace satisfies more and more of our needs that were once met elsewhere, family life takes on what Arlie Hochschild calls an "industrial tone." Playfulness and communal good feeling may be prominent in the office, but at home, time-defined tasks dominate. With Megan's tutoring session over at 5 and her ballet class beginning at 5:15, leaving fifteen minutes for dinner before Josh's basketball practice starts, you half expect some families to adopt the bells or sirens used in early factories. "We're very, very busy people," says a husband and father interviewed in *Father Courage*, a recent study of fathers who share domestic duties with their wives. "We've had to structure [family life] like a business."

For the clearest insight into how ecstatic capitalism has sucked its energy from personal and emotional life, consider the mind-set of the late adolescents and young adults who have grown up in such homes. Their youthful idealism looks familiar enough, but they have transferred that idealism from Big Questions about Life and Love to Career. The Higher Education Research Institute, which has tracked campus attitudes over thirty years, has found that, while in the late 1960s students saw their college years as "a time to develop a meaningful philosophy of life," today they see it as a time to develop their earnings potential. Ben Lieber, dean of students at Amherst College, agrees: "There's one word to describe this generation—driven," he says. "You used to see this among first-generation college students. But over the past five or six years, more and more kids with college-educated parents are looking over their shoulders, 'Who's doing better than I?' There's a pervasive, underlying worry about credentials." "You have the feeling that the days of college as a broad and open-ended contemplation have come to an end," says Oberlin Dean of Students Peter Goldsmith.

Jason Mondberg, the ponytailed, skateboarding CTO of Sparks.com, certainly has no time for such nonsense. "I'm very goal-oriented," he says. "On days off, I always schedule my day. This hour I'll go on a hike, then go snorkeling. I can't lie on a beach." An article in *Fast Company* entitled "Five Ways to Chill; Five Tips to Keep Your Adrenaline Levels from Maxing Out" perfectly captures the current mood; the number one tip, evidently unknown to this generation of working stiffs, is "Look Out the Window."

Thus for the young ecstatic capitalist work is not work, but then leisure is not leisure. And since ecstatic capitalism seems to recognize only one passion, love is not exactly love. University of Chicago professors Amy and Leon Kass frequently ask their students, "What is the most important decision you will make in your life?" The answer is almost invariably "career." When one nonconforming student answered, "the mother of my children," his classmates howled with derision. The casual, no-strings, one-night stand known as the "hook-up" now so common on college campuses, could be labeled Sex That Won't Interfere with Your Career Plans. Yale junior Simon Rodberg, in an article entitled "Woman and Man at Yale," describes the hook-up as "a much needed break from the long-term planning that characterizes so much of our lives." Some of this is a simple matter of the laws of physics. If you are planning a summer internship in New York or law school in Chicago, what do you do with a boyfriend who's joining a start-up in L.A.? Moreover, once students graduate into the real world, the spirit of jokey conviviality that rules at the workplace doesn't necessarily lend itself to deeper involvements. "It's like working at a junior prom all year long," Sparks.com's Allison Behr explained. "But at the end of the day, all of us want a more traditional relationship. There's no time."

Combined with career mania, this time crunch has the effect of suppressing spontaneous human contact, the sort that sometimes leads to unforeseen friendships or romances, and it turns even the young into rigorous, even brutal, pragmatists. When you have a career to pursue, an identity to brand, and a watch to check, someone had better have a pretty fancy pedigree to merit your attention. "Everyone is so motivated and so into control that it's very hard to find someone you think is worth investing time, energy, and sensibility in," a junior from Oakland told Yale student Rodberg.

The Nondisclosure Agreement, a legal document once used by lawyers and CEOs to protect corporate secrets during high-level negotiations and now popular among ambitious young entrepreneurs, is a perfect symbol of the toughening of intimate life. According to the *Wall Street Journal*, some of these young turks are demanding that their friends, roommates, relatives, dinner-party companions, and even their clergymen and fiancées sign on the dotted line, to ensure that if one of them does babble on about his new venture, at least he can sue them for damages. As one consultant told the *Journal*, "It's one of the critical items for a date: car keys, credit cards, condoms, and an NDA."

Still, ecstatic capitalism does not preclude happy endings, especially those in its own image. Take the *New York*

Times wedding announcement of Seth Copeland, chief executive of Wideband Computers and Wideband Semiconductors, and clinical psychology student Stephanie Cantor. The bridegroom said he was attracted to his bride's "cognitive, logical skills," while the bride called theirs a typical Silicon Valley courtship: "The trend is get engaged during lunch and go back to work."

Inevitably, because of the way it colonizes all of life, ecstatic capitalism is bound to suffer some kind of backlash, perhaps during the next downturn. A 1999 *Fast Company* survey showed 91 percent of its respondents believing that it was important to make personal life more of a priority (though 83 percent would choose a ten-thousand-dollar-a-year raise over one more hour a day at home). We're beginning to hear stories of career-driven thirty-year-olds retiring and doing good works in what the *New York Times* has dubbed a "young-life crisis."

The most intense resistance comes from women who, despite the promises of careerist feminism, remain reluctant to surrender so many of their personal urges to the promises of ecstatic work. Writing in the *Wall Street Journal*, Nancy Ann Jeffrey found that many married upper-income women are quitting work and moving back into Friedan's "comfortable concentration camp" of domestic life. Though the number of single-income households has remained steady overall, the proportion has "moved up considerably" among those earning $250,000 or more. Younger women too show signs that they are resisting work's greedy grasp. An Arthur Andersen survey found that teen girls say they'd prefer careers in small business and public service in order to maintain independence. Yalie Rodberg quotes one high school senior girl from Towson, Maryland: "It's funny how many girls are saying, 'You know, I just want to be a housewife now.'" Lisa Belkin, a

Ecstatic Capitalism's Brave New Work Ethic

New York Times reporter covering the work-family beat, wrote of how once during a business trip she sang a lullaby to her two young boys from a telephone bank at the Atlanta airport; the women making calls on both sides of her wept. Some human longings, it seems, resist being cubiclized.

Still, like it or not, for the time being ecstatic capitalism—even when it is less than fully ecstatic—is likely to remain powerful. My boyfriend—now my husband—and I have two children about the age we were when we set out in his Ford Falcon on our spiritual quest to San Francisco. Both of them work hours that would have made us think they are living on a different planet, which in a sense they are. Meanwhile their younger sister, a seventh-grader who rides her scooter to school and still dreams of her Halloween candy, shows little interest in boys—but she is starting to plan her SAT strategy.

[2001]

11

The End of Herstory

When you ask young women today if they think of themselves as feminists, more often than not they will pause for a moment. Then they will answer something like: "Well, I believe in equal pay for equal work," or "Yes, I do believe women should have choices," or "Of course, I believe women should have equal rights."

If these are the principles that define feminism, we are all feminists now. And the future belongs to feminism too: a 2001 *American Demographics* survey of adolescent girls entitled "The Granddaughters of Feminism" found that 97 percent believe women should be paid equally while 92 percent believe "lifestyle choices" should not be limited by sex. Curiously, the war on terror has, if anything, solidified our commitment to women's rights, though orthodox feminists opposed the war as another dangerous example of "the cult of masculinity." The sight of women forced to scurry about in sacks brought home to Americans just how much they treasured their freedoms, including those won for women over the past decades. For a remarkable moment, President Bush and Eleanor Smeal of the Feminist Majority, which had long tried to bring Taliban mistreatment of women to the State Department's attention, seemed to be members of the same party—which, seen against the backdrop of radical Islam, they actually are.

But how do we explain that pause that comes when you ask women if they consider themselves part of the movement? The truth is, very few Americans are capital "F" Feminists. Polls show that only about a quarter of women are willing to accept the label. Younger women seem no more comfortable with the title than their grandmothers were. Marie Wilson, president of the *Ms.* Foundation for Women, has admitted that the elite young women who twenty years ago would have been the generals of the movement are feminists "by attitude . . . [but] are not interested in hearing about organized movements or activism." They mostly do not join NOW or read *Ms.* magazine. They don't think of themselves as second-class citizens of the patriarchy, or follow "women's issues" in the news, and their marital status seems as likely to predict how they will vote as their sex.

Activists who try to make sense of these young feminists who are not Feminists conclude that the movement has an image problem. The reason so many people believe in feminist goals yet reject the label, they say, is that the media have given us a cartoon picture of liberationists as humorless, Birkenstock-wearing man-haters, our era's version of the old-fashioned spinster. Feminism is still an "unfinished revolution," they say, and young women share its goals. They just don't like the packaging.

But this explanation falls far short. Feminism is not simply suffering from a PR problem. It's just over. As in finished.

Supporters will smile and reply that the movement has been read its last rites often during its lifetime. What's different now, though, is that feminism appears not so much dead as obsolete. Yes, it has bred a generation of empowered young women. But rooted in a utopian politics that longs to transcend both biology and ordinary bourgeois longings, it cannot address the realities of the lives that it has helped to change. Young women know this, even if their mothers do not.

Until a year ago, Amanda Laforge could have served as a poster girl for *Ms.* After graduating from Boston University, she went to American University law school. When she married, she kept her maiden name and her job with the Maryland secretary of state. When she got pregnant, she continued commuting forty-five minutes to her new job at the state attorney general's office. When the baby came, she planned to take three months' maternity leave and then return to the office for a continued climb of the career ladder.

It didn't turn out that way. Instead of becoming super career mom, she quit her job. Yet she shows no symptoms of Oppressed Housewife Syndrome. Isn't she bored? "No. I love it." Does she miss her job? "I do miss working—or at least having colleagues. I've started to look for part-time work." Does she worry that she is not her husband's equal? "I feel superior to my husband," she sniffs. "Women are much more powerful." But won't her career suffer? "I'm struggling with this personally right now. I know I've already compromised my ability to reach the height of my career. But I see a lot of room to make up." Is it so easy to put aside her career? "No, but I had friends whose mothers were career women who just got caught up in something. Now they've worked for twenty-five or thirty years for X company, and they didn't get to such enormous heights. Would their lives have been that much different if they had worked part-time? I know a lot of fairly educated people," Amanda concludes, "and no one is looking for more time at the office."

It would be a big mistake to see Amanda as a return to 1950s milk-and-cookies motherhood or as evidence of the backlash that Feminists announce with every article by Katie Roiphe. It would be equally wrong to conclude that most young mothers today are quitting work to be with their babies. Many are; but many others are working part-time, or two days a week at the office, say, and three at home. And, yes, many others are going back to work full-time.

But regardless of how they arrange their lives, women like Amanda illustrate a truth that feminism never anticipated and is still busily denying: after the revolution, women want husbands and children as much as they want anything in life. It's not that the daughters and granddaughters of feminism don't respect those who forgo marriage and motherhood: in the *American Demographics* poll, 89 percent of adolescent girls said a woman does not need a man to be a success, and the percentage of single women between 35 and 44 has increased significantly since 1960. But the vast majority of young women continue to tell pollsters that they want to marry and have children, and they go on to do so. Census experts predict that upward of 90 percent of today's young women will eventually marry, which means, remarkably enough, that women today tie the knot at a rate similar to that of their grandmothers. Moreover, even with the widely publicized decline in fertility in recent decades, a large majority of women will also become mothers; as of 2000, 81 percent of women aged forty to forty-four had given birth to at least one child.

After giving birth, moreover, not many embrace the one preferred Feminist solution to liberated motherhood: dropping the baby off at the day-care center for fifty hours a week. According to another *American Demographics* study, having come from broken or latchkey homes, most Gen-X-ers think the best arrangement is for one parent to stay home with the kids, a belief that other polls suggest the majority of

Americans share. This usually means Mom, even after three decades of feminism and a concerted effort to get fathers to man the nursery. A 1996 Census Bureau report shows that 42 percent of children under five have a parent at home full-time, another 19.4 percent part-time—and the large majority of these parents are women. The latest Census Bureau numbers show that 55 percent of women with infants were in the workforce in 2000, compared with 59 percent two years earlier—the first such decline since 1979.

It's no wonder that Feminists have a hard time accepting that trends like these could represent what women actually want. After all, Feminists of the 1960s and '70s took to the streets on the premise that women wanted to escape from the prison house of the bourgeois home and take up positions in the office and the boardroom, where the real power lies. Women consigned to the role of housewife and mother measured out their days with baby spoons and dirty socks, but work, it seemed to these followers of Betty Friedan, would give them adventure, self-expression, freedom. In the seventies the offices of *Ms.* and other feminist organizations sported signs proclaiming WOMEN WORKING!

Echoes of this kind of thinking still resound in aging Feminist circles. In her 2000 book, *Flux,* for example, Peggy Orenstein explains that work or career "requires the assertion of self," whereas in wifehood and motherhood "your whole identity as a person gets swallowed up." In the same vein, several years ago a successful screenwriter of about fifty told me that she was contemplating divorce. When I expressed sympathetic alarm, she hastened to explain that there was nothing wrong with her marriage; it was just that "I hate that word 'wife.' It's not who I am."

Such talk has about as much resonance as "Remember the *Maine!*" for younger women. For one thing, the romance of work—what might be called the Feminist mystique—has faded. Young women, as more than one I interviewed put it, are far more likely to feel pressure to be "super career women" than to play Ozzie's Harriet. That doesn't mean that those fortunate enough to have challenging jobs don't take great pride in their accomplishments or enjoy the intellectual stimulation they get at the office. And it doesn't mean that there aren't plenty of young women as fiercely ambitious as Duddy Kravitz. But many are put off by the single-minded careerism they associate with Feminism. In *Feminist Fatale: Voices of the Twentysomething Generation Explore the Women's Movement*, Paula Kamen interviewed a number of such skeptics. "There are many women in this field in their late thirties who don't have a family and their entire social life revolves around the job and people [on the job]," says one twentysomething. "I think that's horrible."

Remember also that the majority of women in their twenties and thirties watched their own mothers go to work but didn't see adventurers and heroines. They saw tired women complaining about their bosses and counting the days until the next vacation, just as women their mothers' age saw their fathers doing. And they know from personal experience that taking a meeting with a client or lunching with colleagues involves every bit as much of the role-playing that Feminists wanted to escape. "I worked sixty hours a week from the time I got out of college till I got pregnant," one Boston-area thirty-year-old marketing executive said. "I was tired of it. My job is not emotionally fulfilling. I like it, but it's just a job."

In short, for these women the personal is not political—it's, well . . . personal. Even the most ambitious young women refuse to judge the housewife as, in Betty Friedan's words, a "waste of human self." Sara Ely Hulse, a recently married twenty-six-year-old CBS producer proud of her "independent nature," would seem a logical candidate for Feminist skepticism toward housewifery: her career is so promising that she and her husband consider appointing him the main caregiver when they have children. But when I asked whether she looked down on her mother, who had stayed at home to raise her and her two sisters, she answered heatedly: "Oh God, no! I loved having someone to come home to every day." A young D.C. lawyer-mother I interviewed, though she went back to work three months after giving birth, is also entirely sympathetic to stay-at-homes. After all, when she gets together with friends, she says, "All we talk about is our babies."

Nothing illustrates this reclaiming of the personal more clearly than the Mrs. question. For sixties feminists, becoming Mrs. John Smith epitomized both women's second-class status and their economic and psychological dependence on men. Indeed, former NOW president Patricia Ireland wrote in her recent memoir, *What Women Want*, that a woman taking her husband's name "signifies the loss of her very existence as a person under the law." Pshaw, younger women say; it doesn't mean anything of the sort. You can keep your name if you want—and many women do, as often for practical as for philosophical reasons. You can hyphenate your name or use your maiden name for work and your married name everywhere else. Or if you want to have the same name as your husband and children, go for it. "A lot of women in my office said keeping your maiden name is a hassle, like when the school calls, or the kids' doctor, and asks for you using the child's last name," the independent-minded Sara Hulse said. "I hate hyphenated names—so I changed my name." The D.C. lawyer explained that her decision to use her husband's name was prompted by her experience growing up with a divorced and remarried mother. "I had a different name from my mother," she recalls, "and it always bothered me."

Single women, especially those in their late twenties and early thirties, have other reasons to feel impatient with the Feminist mystique. They followed the careerist script to a tee: they worked until 10 p.m., got flashy jobs, fought for promotions. Meanwhile they had sex when they felt like it, indifferent to whether their partner was husband material or not; they lived with their boyfriends, shrugged when that didn't work out, and moved on to the next one. But after some years of this, many are surprised to find that the single life is less like *Sex and the City* than *The Apartment*.

"Sex is an easily attainable, feminist-approved goal, one that carries less stigma than admitting to loneliness or desperately wanting emotional connection with a man," writes Katherine Marsh in a *Washington Monthly* article, in one of several youthful critiques of Feminism that have recently appeared. "While feminists can solidly advise on how to get rid of a man—obtaining a fair divorce or a restraining order against an abusive spouse—they are fairly mute on how to find love and live with a decent man." Vanessa Grigoriadis, writing in *New York* magazine, tells of a woman whose parents, in thrall to the Feminist career mystique, refused to pay for a wedding if she married before thirty. But now she and her peers are feeling uneasy. "These days, the independence that seemed so fabulous—at least to those of us who tend to use that word a lot—doesn't anymore."

These younger women are especially peeved that, in promoting female independence, Feminism denied biological realities that now loom large. Feminists often like to talk about the "click"—the moment when a woman experiences discrimination so clearly that she sees her whole life in a radically new light. For a lot of younger women, the "click" moment has now arrived in a totally unexpected form. With the torrent of media coverage following the recent publication of Sylvia Ann Hewlett's *Creating a Life*—publicity that focused on the fertility problems of older high-achieving women—everything looks different. For just as there are no atheists in foxholes, there are no Feminists in the throes of fertility anxiety.

"I'm twenty-eight and grew up in Manhattan, attended a competitive private high school and a liberal-arts college," marvels Grigoriadis, "and at no point did anyone bring up the notion that the sexes were anything but equal. To me, it seemed like ideology was going to triumph over biology." The "unwillingness to confront the personal—more precisely the feminine personal—is the biggest failure of the Second Wave," Sara Blustain, the thirty-two-year-old managing editor of the *New Republic*, has written. ("Second Wave" feminism is sixties and seventies feminism; First Wavers were the suffragettes.) "It's why the movement has refused to deal with the fact that even *after* the Revolution, many women want to marry men and bear their children. . . . It's why, just this month, *Time* ran on its cover another installment of the Baby vs. Career story that drove women I know to tears for reminding us of the incredible double bind."

Even young women who embrace the Feminist label have a beef with Sisterly avoidance of "the feminine personal." Susan Jane Gilman, author of *Kiss My Tiara: How to Rule the World as a Smartmouth Goddess*, is one of Feminism's more dutiful daughters in many ways—her pet issues include abortion rights, sexual harassment, and domestic violence—yet she says: "For women today, feminism is often perceived as dreary. As elitist, academic, Victorian, whiny, and passé." Young women Gilman's age don't remember the thrill of the bra-burning, let's-do-it-in-the-road seventies; instead they went to the thin-lipped, Catherine MacKinnon school of Feminism, where they learned that even their younger brothers were potential harassers, even rapists. They're having none of it. Calling themselves girlie feminists, lipstick feminists, or sometimes just Third Wavers, they have taken to flaunting the very femininity that Feminists had scolded would lead men to objectify them.

If there is a beauty myth, these renegades are true believers. They want their lip gloss, their Victoria's Secret lingerie, and their MTV. Oxford student Chelsea Clinton, pictured recently cuddling with her boyfriend in a Venetian gondola and at a Paris fashion show with a deep décolletage and enough mascara to paint a fence, appears to be a girlie feminist. At her age, her mother sported geeky glasses and unkempt hair, emblems of the I've-got-more-important-things-on-my-mind-than-attracting-a-man branch of Feminism, the Second Wave incarnate.

Still, it is more than nail polish that makes these daughters very different from what their mothers envisioned when they groomed them to take over the family business. For all their in-your-face sexual bravado, girlie feminists can be unabashed traditionalists. Consider *Bust*, a girlie Internet 'zine that describes itself as "the magazine for women with something to get off their chests." With its signature T-shirts that say KISS MY ASS and TOUGH TITTIES, and its pronouncement of "The New Girl Order," *Bust* is full of Erica Jongish, zipless-sex Attitude. Yet as the title of one article, "A Bad Girl's Guide to Good Housekeeping," suggests, the hipness coexists with more conventional desires. A recent chat-room offering, "A Feminist Analysis of the Baby Scare," was less MacKinnon than *Bride*. "I'm conflicted," one participant wrote, "Did some feminist drop the ball on this one? Have we understated the power of biology?" Another contributor was just mad: "I am not a mother and I am still not sure if/when I will be one," she wrote. "But it really depresses me that if I do choose to get knocked up before the age of 30, that I will be looked upon as nothing more than a tool of the patriarchy. Sisterhood is powerful. Baloney."

What all this suggests is a vast and sharper-than-a-serpent's-tooth generation gap between Feminists and their progeny. "A woman in her twenties or thirties and I are in parallel universes, as if we were in two different countries," Gloria Steinem has admitted. Being the out-of-touch old-timers is especially painful for aging boomer-Feminists, once so proud of being in the vanguard. In the course of research-ing her recent history of the women's movement, Susan Brownmiller looked up many old activist acquaintances and found them "very depressed" at their irrelevance. Other Sec-ond Wavers get prickly: how can these youngsters be so igno-rant of what is at stake here?

Lisa Belkin, a *New York Times* reporter who covers the "work-family" beat and frequently recounts her own at-tempts to balance her enviable career with two young sons and a husband, was recently on the receiving end of this irri-tability, when Maureen Corrigan, a boomer Georgetown lit-erature professor, reviewed her recent collection of columns, *Life's Work*. Corrigan blasted the younger woman's failure to show more respect for the Second Wave legacy. Where Belkin cheerfully accepts the inevitable tensions between her career and family life, Corrigan spies the "small pathologies of an unfinished revolution." Where the frankly ambitious Belkin nevertheless acknowledges that the stresses of her husband's job as a pediatric cardiologist make her own dead-line pressures seem less intense, Corrigan frets that young women should "stop apologizing for having professional ambitions and minds of their own." And when Belkin describes the confusion that sometimes comes from using her maiden name at work and her husband's name socially, Corrigan explodes: this young woman has a "weirdly reactionary split personality," she snarls. "Why [did] she choose to create problems for herself by taking her husband's last name in the first place?"

Meanwhile the younger generation concludes that older women just don't get it. Peggy Orenstein, who in her late thirties is old enough to be a card-carrying member of the Sisterhood but young enough to know that the future needs attending to, traveled around the country asking two hundred women about their attitudes toward work, romance, and family for her book, *Flux*. She was puzzled to find women who share neither her passion for work nor her ambivalence toward marriage and motherhood. During the question period after a speech at Washington University, a student burst out: "I don't want to have to wait until I'm thirty-five to have kids!" Orenstein's priceless reaction speaks volumes about the chasm between the New Girl Order and the Second Wave Old Guard. "I nodded too, sympathetically. It really wasn't fair. Then suddenly, I thought, 'Wait a minute! I'm nearly thirty-seven and I don't have children yet. These women don't want to be *me*.'"

Of course, many older Feminists are shocked—*shocked!*—that their daughters' generation could think that they looked down their noses at the feminine personal. "The notion that the women's movement denigrates women who choose the traditional roles of wife and mother is arrant nonsense," columnist Molly Ivins states emphatically. She might want to sign up for a few women's studies classes at Yale or the University of Texas or check out the current literature from NOW. What she'll find is not just hostility to "tra-

ditional roles" but a tight-wound ambivalence toward the biological urges that young women now so loudly affirm and a
hostility to bourgeois life that few young women share.

Take the Feminist attitude toward marriage. When college women sit at the knee of their female elders, they may
well read from the widely used textbook *Women's Realities,
Women's Choices.* There they will learn that "the institution
of marriage and the role of 'wife' are intimately connected
with the subordination of women in society in general." For
the teachers, this attitude isn't just theoretical. Daphne Patai,
co-author of *Professing Feminism* and author of *Heterophobia,* books critical of the women's studies industry, recounts
a lunch with other female academics at which one announces she is getting married. The response: shocked, dead,
embarrassed silence.

Yet Feminist hostility to marriage goes beyond the view
that it makes women second-class citizens. Feminists also
cling to the idea of the post-bourgeois liberated woman who
not only doesn't need a man but also rejects conventional
middle-class life in favor of a self-created, adventurous independence. When Gloria fish-without-a-bicycle Steinem married in 2000, for example, she evidently felt she had to lend
her act a heroic, anti-bourgeois cast. "I had no desire to get
married and neither did he," she said—but "it seems rebellious at 66."

Motherhood too interests orthodox Feminists only inso-
far as it overturns bourgeois norms. NOW, for example,
fiercely supports single welfare mothers and bristles at any
reform that might try to encourage them to go to regular
jobs or—God forbid—to marry. Ireland got herself arrested
at a 1996 demonstration at the Capitol when the House
passed "the Republican welfare bill that would have plunged
millions of women and children deeper into poverty," as she

put it in her memoir. Though child poverty and overall poverty have declined since welfare reform, NOW has failed to acknowledge its error. In addition, the group continues to sound the alarm against current proposals to promote marriage. As Kim Gandy, the current NOW president, says, the plan reminds her of her backward "grandmother's friends say[ing], 'Honey, when are you going to get married?'"

Still, the NOW folks can believe in the happily-ever-after as long as they're talking about lesbians. NOW heavily promotes gay marriage and adoption—not, like other advocates, as a civil rights issue, but because they view lesbian liaisons and motherhood as a means of subverting conventional marriage and sex roles. Norah Vincent, a *Los Angeles Times* columnist and a gay libertarian, dismisses the organization's support. "It's the old Marxist agenda. Feminists see gay people as the newest proletariat. They want to overthrow the old bourgeois system. It's not my agenda." She adds that she and her girlfriend often joke that they would love nothing more than a traditional middle-class life. "We think of advertising: 'Two women willing to do housework and take care of children in return for a husband.'"

But while Feminists can get as misty as a Hallmark card over lesbian and welfare mothers, they cast a colder eye upon the other 90 percent of women who might look longingly inside Snuglis and baby carriages. Phyllis Chesler, author of the Second Wave best-seller *Women and Madness*, recounts that, when she became pregnant in the late seventies, friends begged her not to have a child, which would cause her to abandon the movement. These days, when faced with young female baby hunger, Second Wavers are still acting as skittish as Hugh Hefner. Last fall, for example, alarmed at infertility problems they were seeing in the increasing number of women putting off childbearing into their forties, the American Society for Reproductive Medicine launched an ad campaign warning that "Advancing Age Decreases Your Ability to Have Children." But where the doctors were focusing on the gap they observed between medical fact and wishful thinking on the part of contemporary women, one that had already brought many to grief, the Feminists spied only the ever-lurking bourgeois backlash against the heroic career woman. "There is an anti-feminist agenda that says we should go back to the 1950s," Caryl Rivers, a professor of journalism at Boston University and a frequent commentator on Feminist issues, pronounced in *Time*. "The subliminal message is 'Don't get too educated; don't get too successful or too ambitious.'"

And here we come to the primary reason for Feminism's descent into irrelevance. Whereas most young women will at some point want babies like they want food, for Feminists, motherhood is the ten-ton boulder in the path of genuine liberation. It mucks up ambition, turning fabulous heroines of the workplace—killer lawyers, 24/7 businesswomen, and ruthless senator wannabes—into bourgeois wifies and mommies. It hinders absolute equality, since women with children don't usually crash through glass ceilings. They resist traveling three days a week to meet with hotshot clients; they look at their watches frequently and make a lot of personal phone calls.

Nothing irks a movement Feminist more than news of a Sister packing in a high-powered career. Candice Carpenter, who when she married left her position as CEO of iVillage, changed her name, and joined the ranks of stay-at-home mothers, earned the wrath of Brandeis professor Linda Hirshman, who called her "the born-again Stepford wife." When presidential aide Karen Hughes announced that she was leaving Washington because her family was "homesick" for Texas, Hirshman was equally incensed, blasting Hughes's husband for not "supporting her career" and for failing to promote "justice in the private world of the family."

Feminists deal in two ways with the unsettling fact that, even after the revolution, women persist in wanting to be mothers. The first tack is simple denial. Amazingly, given young women's preoccupation with how to balance work and motherhood, neither NOW nor the Feminist Majority, the movement's two most influential organizations, includes maternity leave, flextime, or even day care on its list of vital issues.

The other tack, favored by academic Feminists, is a more complex denial. Yes, women may want babies, they concede; but that doesn't mean they want motherhood—at least not motherhood as it has been "constructed" by the patriarchy throughout history. For these theorists, only a social arrangement that makes men and women exactly equal co-parents—at work precisely the same number of hours, and taking care of the children precisely the same number of hours—is acceptable. In an article in the *American Prospect*, Janet Gornick averaged out the number of hours worked by mothers of children under three (23) and those worked by fathers (44) and proclaimed the egalitarian goal: both Mom and Dad should work 33.5 hours a week. It is not enough to give men and women more flexibility and choices about how to organize their lives; the goal is "unbending gender," as American University law professor Joan Williams puts it in her book of that title. Williams rejects what she calls "choice rhetoric"; a woman who thinks she is freely choosing to stay home is just fooling herself, in thrall to the "ideology of domesticity."

Feminists who share Williams's and Gornick's goals aren't about to let biology get in the way of their plans for utopian parity. Though they don't go as far as those 1970s radicals who looked forward to growing fetuses outside the womb, they search for ways to make every aspect of motherhood a fifty-fifty proposition. In *Woman: An Intimate Geography*, for instance, Natalie Angie comes up with one idea about "sharing" breastfeeding: if the father would just rock the baby between feedings "against his naked breast," then men too could have "a visceral connection with a newborn."

Little wonder that few women in their twenties and thirties seek to complete this so-called unfinished revolution. They don't yearn for the radical transformation of biological restraints and bourgeois aspirations devoutly wished by stalwarts. Even those few who want more androgynous sex roles for themselves don't wish to impose them on others. Yes, they took women's studies courses—often only to satisfy their college's diversity requirement—but they came away unimpressed. To many of them, Feminism today represents not liberation but its opposite: a life that must be lived according to a strict, severe ideology. The younger generation, on the other hand, wants a liberation "that isn't just freedom to choose [but] . . . freedom from having to justify one's choices," as Jennifer Foote Sweeney has put it in *Salon*. In short, they're ready to depoliticize the personal.

But none of this means that the second sex is entirely at peace in the New Girl—or the New Woman—Order. There is a deep tension between young family values and female ambition that will spark many years of cultural debate—and it's not just about who's going to do the laundry or take the kids to the pediatrician. There is still plenty of grumbling on that score, of course: in her recent study *For Better or For Worse*, for example, Mavis Hetherington found that two-thirds of married women complained about the disproportionate burden of house and child care that falls on their shoulders (though she also found that traditional families, with bread-winner husband and stay-at-home wife, had the lowest rate of divorce).

But more important, biology simply disagrees with our careerist culture. The evidence is that, even after thirty years of the Feminist mystique, women may want men to help out more, but they still want to be the primary parent and nester-in-chief. *The Motherhood Report*, a 1989 survey of over one thousand mothers, found that, while three-quarters of women want men to pitch in more, their goal is not fifty-fifty parenting. They like being boss at home. Suzanne Bran Levine's 2000 *Father Courage: What Happens When Men Put Family First* suggests that in this department not much has changed in the past ten years. Levine went searching for "the second stage of the gender role revolution"—couples who defy all traditional mommy-daddy divisions. She found some who, with much struggling, were doing so (though you don't have to be Robert Young to think that her description of the brutal, dawn-to-midnight, pass-the-baton existence of some of her couples—think of it as X-treme domesticity—makes *Father Knows Best* look like a sane alternative). But she also finds, contrary to the Feminist picture of the patriarchy foisting unwanted roles on women, that it is often the second sex who, wanting to be the first sex in the nursery, undermines these arrangements.

In my own interviews I found that young women are not especially nervous about thinking of this stubborn clinging to traditional roles as based in biology. When you ask if there are innate differences between the sexes, they talk comfortably in some of the terms that would satisfy an evolutionary psychologist. They generally believe that women have a closer bond with babies. They see that women usually play what one thirtyish lawyer called "household executive." And they're not especially worried about it. "I don't see it as injustice unless [women] are denied opportunity," one lawyer shrugged. As Norah Vincent concludes, "Equal does not mean the same."

The sharpest tension in the lives of the post-Feminist young comes from a workplace designed for people who can put in long, consecutive hours—mainly men and childless women. Mothers, as well as many fathers, want jobs with more flexibility through job sharing, part-time hours, and leaves of absence. And they want the assurance that they can get back on the fast track when the demands of child-rearing ease off. More discussion and lobbying about these issues in the future is certain. Right now, for instance, Ann Crittenden, the author of *The Price of Motherhood*, is launching a lobbying group called MOTHER (Mothers Ought to Have Equal Rights), dedicated to promoting more family-friendly workplaces, improved benefits for mothers, and a reduction of the "mommy tax."

Still, this tension can't be entirely, or even mostly, resolved. The difficult truth is that the very economy that stirs the imaginations and ambitions of young people—that makes them work eighty hours a week in a start-up business, that makes them want to learn new skills or take on extra duties so that they can get promoted or start their own businesses—is the same economy that will never be especially family-friendly and that often leaves even ambitious working mothers behind. Those who long for the Western European model, with its shorter workweeks, longer vacation times, and generous maternity and paternity leaves, fail to see that those more regulated economies also produce less excitement, less creativity, less opportunity, less money, less of what I've called "ecstatic capitalism." Western European workers don't work as hard; they also don't have as many opportunities to create new businesses, develop new skills, and get rich.

Many women seem to understand this reality. A number of those I interviewed said that their crisis-driven jobs made part-time hours either impossible or a sure route to less interesting assignments. They did not blame their employers; they were quick to admit that if you tell clients that the person handling their case or account won't be in on Tuesdays, Wednesdays, and Fridays, you're going to lose them. All of the co-parenting fathers in Levine's book have had to give up not just Saturday golf but also dreams of writing a novel or of making partner in the firm. In such marriages, women are not the only ones who can't have it all. To these couples, everybody wins—Levine's male subjects appear pleased with how close they are to their children; but everybody loses too.

The more immediate point, however, is that while younger women are struggling with how to balance work and family, they have said goodbye to the radical dreams of Feminism. Case in point: Rachel Foster, a Brooklyn mother of two young children who is on leave from her job as a Legal Aid lawyer. Foster is the great-granddaughter of William Foster, the founder of the American Communist party, and his wife Esther Peterson, a once well-known free-love nudist, who raised Rachel's grandfather in an anarchist community. She is the daughter of a social-worker mother who worked from the time Rachel was five weeks old. Foster expects to return eventually to "social justice and advocacy." But right now, as the largely content stay-at-home wife of a real estate developer, one thing's for sure: she's not looking to live like her great-grandparents.

[2002]

Index

Abraham, Nathaniel, 94
Abstinence education, xvii, 130
Addams Family, The, 37
Adler, Patricia A., 99
Adler, Peter, 99
"Adolescent society," 85
Adolescents: and alienation, 109;
    stress, 162, 163, 164
Aesop, 45
Albertini, Christine, 154
Albright College, 143
Aliquippa Middle School, 81
All Souls Unitarian, 29
Allen-Stevenson (private school),
    21
Alloy, Jim, 102, 106
AM Cosmetics, 91
American Association of School
    Administrators, 75
American Child Pastoral, 56, 62,
    65, 68, 70
American Communist party, 189
"American cool," xvii, 124
American Cool (Stearns), 124
American Demographics, 170,
    173
American Girl, 87, 89
American Prospect, 185
American Society for
    Reproductive Medicine, 184

Amherst College, 140, 143, 166
Androcles, 42
Angels in the Outfield, 91
Angier, Natalie, 186
Antioch College, 133
Apartment, The, 177
Arc Consulting, 89
Are You the One for Me?
    (DeAngelis), 124
Arendt, Hannah, 100
Aristotle, 86
Arnette, June, 83
Arrested Development, 46
Ashbrook, Tom, 155, 156
Atkinson, Ti-Grace, 125
Authentic self, 62; and parental
    authority, 64; self-restraint,
    63
Authority: collapse of, 85, 106;
    resistance of, 68; suspicion
    of, 64; under attack, 76;
    undermining of, 79

Baby and Child Care (Spock), 56
"Baby Ivies" (private elementary
    schools), xiii, 21, 22, 23, 28
Backstreet Boys, 87
Barney, 44
Bay Ridge (N.Y.), 23

Index

Bazarini, Ronald, 25
Beach Boys, 37
Beatles, 88
Bedford (N.Y.), 102, 106
Behr, Allison, 153, 167
Belkin, Lisa, 168, 180, 181
Bell, Daniel, 157, 158
Bellamy, Edward, 157
Belsky, Jay, 6, 7
Berger, Peter and Brigitte, 157
Berkeley Carroll (private school), 27, 88
Bettelheim, Bruno, 15, 16, 43, 44
Beverly Hills 90210, 135
Blige, Mary J., 134
Bloom, Benjamin, 47
Blustain, Sara, 178
Bobos in Paradise (Brooks), 158
Bonne Bell cosmetics, 104
Books That Build Character, 45
Boston University, 142, 184
Boys: A Schoolmaster's Journal (Bazarini), 25
Brand Called You, The (Peters), 155
Brandeis Review, 143
Brazelton, T. Berry, 57, 58, 66
Brearley (private school), 21, 22
Brick Church, 22, 29
Bride, 179
Brooklyn Friends (private school), 23
Brooks, David, 158
Brown, Lyn Mikel, 70
Brown University, 140
Brownmiller, Susan, 180
Buckley (private school), 21, 34
Bureau of Labor Statistics, 11
Bush, George W., 170
Bust, 179
Byoir, Carl, 49

Cantor, Stephanie, 168
Capitalism, xviii, 12, 151, 152, 153, 156, 160, 164, 166, 188;

backlash against, 168; intimate relationships, effect on, 164, 166; women, attitude toward, 13, 168
Carey, Mariah, 134
Carnegie Corporation, 36, 47
Carnegie Foundation for the Advancement of Teaching, 52
Carnegie Mellon University, 142
Carpenter, Candice, 184
Cash, Johnny, 38
Castle, Caroline, 45
Center for Research on the Influences of Television on Children, 36, 51
Chapin (girls' school), 20, 21, 28, 29
Chappaqua (N.Y.), 24
Chesler, Phyllis, 183
Ch!ckaboom, 89
Chicago (Ill.), 85, 86, 161
Child care. *See* Day care.
Child Care Action Campaign, 14
Child empowerment, 105, 106, 107
Child rearing, 55, 57; and discipline, 16, 66; the workplace, conflicts in, 188
Children: and achievement of, 33; capitalism, effect on, 162; civilizing process, 54, 55, 58, 63, 70, 71; discipline of, 66; empathy, 59, 60, 61; manners, teaching of, 63; morality, 55, 59, 60, 62, 65, 67, 68, 69; self-restraint, development of, 55, 56; socialization of, 17, 18, 85; stress of, 32; temper tantrums, 58, 59
Children and Television: Lessons from Sesame Street (Lesser), 48
Children Now, 113
Children's Defense Fund, 14

Index

Children's Health and Executive
    Club, 161
Children's Television Workshop
    (CTW), 35, 46, 49, 50, 51, 52
Choate (private school), 21
Christian Science Monitor, 5
Christie, Ellen, 93
Chubb, John, 84
"Cinderella," 44, 45
Clarke-Stewart, Alison, 8, 17
Clinton, Chelsea, 179
Clinton, Hillary, 150
Cohen, Michael, 89
Cole, Paula, 87
Coleman, James, 85
Coles, Robert, 65, 66
College: curriculum, 138, 139,
    141, 165, 166; model
    student, portrait of, 143;
    requirements, lack of, 140,
    142, 144; and shopping-mall
    curriculum, 146
Collegiate (private school), 21,
    25, 30, 31
Colon, Jeff, 161
Columbine, xii, 73, 83, 108, 117;
    and middle-class culture,
    109; nihilism, 116
Colvin, Helen, 101
Coming of Age in New Jersey
    (Moffatt), 141
Communiqué, 81, 82
Connecticut College, 144
Container Store, The, 159
Cook, Thomas, 50
Cooney, Joan Ganz, 36, 37, 47,
    48, 52
Copeland, Seth, 168
Corporation for Public
    Broadcasting, 36
Corrigan, Maureen, 180, 181
CosmoGIRL, xvi
Cosmopolitan, 135
Crawford, Cindy, 135
Creating a Life (Hewlett), 178
Crème de la Crème day-care

center (Houston), 3, 4
Crittenden, Ann, 9, 10, 13, 188
*Cultural Contradictions of
    Capitalism, The* (Bell), 157
Culture of Narcissism, The
    (Lasch), 137
Curtis, Jamie Lee, 38

Dallas Morning News, 162
Dalton (private school), 21, 22,
    28
Damon, Matt, 87
Damon, William, 60
*Davis v. Monroe County School
    District*, 82
Dawson's Creek, 112
Day care, xiii, xiv, 3, 4; and
    aggressive behavior, 4, 5, 6,
    16, 17, 18; children, long-
    term effects on, 6, 7, 13, 14;
    motherhood, effect on, 9,
    10; as preschool, 14;
    underclass children, effects
    on, 17
DeAngelis, Beverly, 124
Delia, 89
Depp, Johnny, 93
Deritis, Susan, 11
Des'ree, 123, 124
Details, 135
Dialectic of Sex, The (Firestone),
    125
DiCaprio, Leonardo, 87, 92
Discipline, 73; in schools, 76;
    and self-esteem, of children,
    103
Dogmatic Wisdom (Jacoby), 138
Doherty, William, 32
Domingo, Placido, 37
Donahue, 132
"Dyslexic Heart," 123

Early childhood, and attitudes
    toward, 20

Index

Early Steps, 24
Ecompany, 159
Ecstatic capitalism. *See* Capitalism.
Educational Records Bureau (ERB), 26, 27, 28
Educational television, 36, 48, 49, 51
Educational Testing Service (ETS), 50
Egotism, in American life, 67
Elders, Joycelyn, 134
Elias, Norbert, 54
Emerson, Ralph Waldo, 148
Emotional Life of the Toddler, The, 59
Empathy, 59, 60
ER, 13
Erikson, Erik, 120
Erotic Wars (Rubin), 131
Esquire, 126
Estefan, Gloria, 38
Eugene Lang College of the New School, 142–143
Ewen, Danielle, 14

Families and Work Institute, 153
Fast Company, 151, 152, 154, 158, 163, 166, 168
Father Courage: What Happens When Men Put Family First (Levine), 165, 187
Father Knows Best, 187
Feminine Mystique, The (Friedan), 158
Feminism, xix; and adolescent girls, 170, 176; day care, attitude toward, 7; First Wave, 178; marriage, 182; middle-class life, attitude toward, 182; motherhood, 173, 174, 178, 182, 184, 185, 187; as obsolete, 171; rational love vs. romantic love, 124, 125, 132; Second Wave, 178, 179, 180, 181, 183; Third Wave, 179; work, attitude toward, 158, 175; young women, attitude toward, 171, 172, 174, 175, 177, 178, 179, 180, 182, 186, 189
Feminist Fatale: Voices of the Twentysomething Generation Explore the Women's Movement (Kamen), 175
Feminist Majority, 170, 185
Fieldston (private school), 21, 25
Finn, Huck, 56
Firestone, Shulamith, 125
Fisher, William A., 129
Flexible work hours, 6, 7
Flipper, 47
Flux (Orenstein), 158, 174, 181
For Better or For Worse (Hetherington), 186
Fortas, Abe, 76
Fortune, 155, 159
Foster, Rachel, 189
Foster, William, 189
Four Tops, 37
Fox Lane Middle School, 102
Franklin and Marshall, 143, 147
Freaks and Geeks, 85
French, Marilyn, 125
Freud, Sigmund, 61, 124, 136, 157
Friedan, Betty, 158, 168, 174, 175
Friedman, Sarah, 7, 8
Friend, Bruce, 89
Friends Seminary (private school), 21, 22
Frontline, 109, 110, 114, 120
"Fulbright Scholars," 74

Galen, Laura, 92
Gandy, Kim, 183
Gelfand, Donna, 62
Gender Stereotype, 13

Index

Generation X, 155; and
    motherhood, 174
Gerstel, Jeffrey, 78
Gilligan, Carol, 67, 69, 70, 71,
    72, 103, 104
Gilman, Susan Jane, 178
Girl Scouts of America, 93
Girls, and self-esteem, loss of,
    70, 71, 103, 104, 105
*Girls and Young Women
    Entrepreneurs: True Stories
    About Starting and Running
    a Business*, 162
Goldberg, Danny, 92
Golden, Andrew, 94
Golden Gate Park, 150
Golden Rule, 68
Golding, William, 110
Goldman, Victoria, 21
Goldsmith, Peter, 166
Good Housekeeping, 130
Gornick, Janet, 185
Goss v. Lopez, 77, 78, 79
Grace Church (private school),
    21
Granados, Maggie, 27
Green Acres (Fla.), 74
Greening of America, The
    (Reich), 157
Gretarsson, Sigurdur, 62
Grigoriadis, Vanessa, 177, 178
Grinnell College, 140, 146
Groton (private school), 21
Guilt, 61, 62
Gun-Free Schools Act, 79

Habits of the Heart, 147
Haight-Ashbury, 150, 158
Hanson, 92
Harriet the Spy, 91
Harrisburg (Pa.), 101
Harvard Business Review, 9
Harvard University, 140
Head Start, 5, 47
"Headmaster's Circle, The," 25

Hefner, Hugh, 183
Henson, Jim, 48
Heritage High School, 117
"Hero," 134
Hersch, Patricia, 100
Heterophobia (Patai), 182
Hetherington, Mavis, 186
Hewitt (private school), 25, 26,
    34
Hewlett, Sylvia Ann, 178
Higher Education Research
    Institute, 165
Hirshman, Linda, 184, 185
Hochschild, Arlie, 153, 165
Hoffman, Martin, 60, 61
Hogan, Christie, 95, 98
Homeless Mind, The (Berger and
    Berger), 157
Horace Mann (private school),
    21, 22, 25
Howells, William Dean, 157
Hughes, Karen, 184, 185
Hulse, Sara Ely, 175, 176
Hunnicutt, Benjamin, 157
Hunter, Bruce, 75
Huston, Aletha C., 50–51
Hyde Park (Chicago), xi, xiv

Identity, 62
In a Different Voice (Gilligan), 69
Individualism, xvii, 124, 147;
    excesses of, 17–18; past, as
    barrier to self-fulfillment,
    148; radical, 67, 72
Individuals with Disabilities
    Education Act (IDEA), 74,
    75, 79
Ireland, Patricia, 176, 182
Islam, 171
Israel, 35
Ivins, Molly, 181

Jackson, Jesse, 73
Jacoby, Russell, 138

Index

Jaffe, Stanley, 92
Jaws, 37
Jewel, 89
"John Henry," 44
Johnson, Robert L., 97
Jonesboro (Ark.), 94, 109
Jong, Erica, 133
Jordache Jeans, 101

Kaiser Foundation, 112, 113, 114
Kamen, Paula, 175
Kapetanakes, Barbara, 90
Kass, Amy and Leon, 166
Kattiman, Libby Peszyk, 91
"Keep Schools Safe," 80
Kermit the Frog, 44
Kibbutz, 15, 16
Kidscape, 94
Kindergarten, 19, 20, 23, 27; and IQ testing, 26; tuition of, 24
Kindlon, Dan, 96
Kiss My Tiara: How to Rule the World as a Smartmouth Goddess (Gilman), 178
Kohlberg, Lawrence, 67, 68; and nature's law, 69
Kolodny, Nancy, 96
Krausman, Jeff, 76, 77
KREM-TV, 3

Labor movement, 157
Laforge, Amanda, 172
Lakewood (Calif.), 137
"Language for Tots," 31
Lasch, Christopher, 137, 158
Latchkey kids, 98
Lauper, Cyndi, 37
Laurel School (Cleveland), 70
Leach, Penelope, xv, 57, 58, 64, 65
Leap, The (Ashbrook), 155
Lesser, Gerald, 48

Levine, Suzanne Bran, 187, 189
Lewis, Julie, 75, 79
Lieber, Ben, 165
Life's Work (Belkin), 180
Limited Too, 89
Lindau, Felicia, 164
"Little Red Riding Hood," 44
Little Red Schoolhouse (private school), 21
Littleton (Colo.), 108, 110, 117
Looking Backward (Bellamy), 157
Lord of the Flies (Golding), 70, 110
Los Angeles Times, 7, 183
"Lost Children of Rockdale County, The," 109–110, 111, 112, 117; and loneliness, 111, 113; values, imparting of, 114, 115
Loudon County (Va.), xi
Louisville (Ky.), 95
Love, 124; as civilizing force, 126; courtly love, 126; emotional alienation, 137; individualism, 131
"Love" (essay), 122
Lowey, Nita, 36

MacFarquhar, Larissa, 164
MacKinnon, Catherine, 179
Mad About You, 123
Madeline, 91, 92
Mademoiselle, 122
Madonna, 20, 37, 38
Magaziner, Ira, 140
Making Cents: Every Kid's Guide to Money, 162
Manhattan Family Guide to Private Schools, The (Goldman), 21, 25
Manners, 63
Marland, Sidney, 36
Marsh, Katherine, 177
Marymount (private school), 21

Index

Massachusetts Department of Public Health, 128
Materialism, 151
McCain, John, 82
McNeal, James U., 162
McVeigh, Timothy, 17
Meeting at the Crossroads (Gilligan), 70, 71
Mercury Records, 92
Miami (Fla.), 90
Mickens, Frank, 83
MicroStrategy, 164
Middle-class, and spiritual void, 109, 110, 121
Midler, Bette, 38
Mighty Morphin Power Rangers, 36
Minow, Newton, 47
Mister Rogers, 42, 49
Mitchell, Juliet, 125
Moe, Terry, 84
Moffatt, Michael, 141, 145, 146
"Mommy Track," 9, 11, 18
Mondberg, Jason, 166
Moral Child: Nurturing Children's Natural Moral Growth, The (Damon), 60, 68
Moral Intelligence of Children, The (Coles), 65, 68
Morality, 55, 60, 67; and culture, effects on, 16, 18; feminine version of, 69; and girls, 70, 71; manners, 68; moral development, 67, 68; moral instruction, 65, 66; nonjudgmentalism, 114; as self-restraint, 61; shared values, community of, 82, 83
Morrisett, Lloyd, 47, 48
Moss, Kate, 96
Motherhood, 173; and business world, attitude toward, 9; career, conflict with, 10; guilt, 10; as primary caretakers, 12; and the workplace, 11, 12

Motherhood Report, The, 187
Mothers at Home, 11
Mothers Ought to Have Equal Rights (MOTHER), 188
Motown, 37
Mozambique, 35
Ms., 171, 172, 174
Ms. Foundation for Women, 171
MTV, xvi
Muppets, 37, 38, 39, 42, 48
Museum of Modern Art, 35

National Association for the Education of Young Children, 10
National Association of Scholars, 141
National Association of School Psychologists, 81
National Attorneys General, 80
National Institute of Child Health and Development (NICHD), 4, 6, 7, 8, 9, 10, 15, 17
National Longitudinal Study of Adolescent Health, 162
National Organization of Women (NOW), 171, 176, 181, 182, 185; gay marriage, support of, 183; welfare reform, 182, 183
National School Boards Association, 75–76, 79, 80
National School Safety Center, 83
Netp@rk, 160
New economy, 151, 153, 154; and children, 161, 162; spiritual dimension of, 155, 156; stress, 163
New Jersey Coalition for Battered Women, 125
New Kids on the Block, 92
New Republic, 178
New York, and school system, 24

Index

New York magazine, 135, 163, 177
New York Times, 8, 10, 11, 90, 102, 159, 161, 162, 168
New York Times Guide to New York City Private Schools, The, 22
New York Woman, 9
New Yorker, 164
Newsweek, 11, 14, 160
Nicholson, Bellen, 26, 27, 33
Nickelodeon, 89
Nickelodeon (magazine), 92
Nickelodeon-Yankelovich Youth Monitor, 89
Nietzsche, Friedrich, 124, 155
Nightingale-Bamford (private school), 21
Nin, Anaïs, 133
92nd Street YMHA, 23
Nondisclosure Agreement, 167
Nursery schools, 23, 26, 27; admission process, 27–28, 29, 30, 31; precurricular activities, 30–31

Oberlin College, 166
Object of My Affection, 92
Occidental, 140
Odysseus, 44
Office of Juvenile Justice and Delinquency Prevention, 94
One Life to Live, 135
Oprah, 132
Orenstein, Peggy, 7, 103, 158, 174, 181
Organization Man, 158
Orwin, Clifford, 55

Paglia, Camille, 134, 140
Parental authority, 64
Parental leave, 6, 7
Parents: and moral awareness, lack of, 112; teenagers,

relationships with, 112
Patai, Daphne, 182
Peer Power: Culture and Identity (Adler and Adler), 99
Peer pressure, 33, 97, 99, 100, 102
Pelzer, Jackie, 24
Pennoyer, Russell, 25
Perlman, Itzhak, 37
Person in Need of Supervision (PINS), 106
Peters, Tom, 155
Peterson, Esther, 189
Philadelphia Inquirer, 18
Pianta, Robert, 8
Plato, 18, 55
Playboy, 126
Politics, Markets and American Schools (Chubb and Moe), 84
Poly Prep (private school), 23
Pontiac (Mich.), 94
Popular, 85
"Poverty, Anti-Poverty, and the Poor," 47
Preadolescent. *See* Tweens.
"Preparing the Workers of Tomorrow: A Report on Early Learning," 14
Preschool, 14
Presley, Elvis, 37, 88
Price of Motherhood, The (Crittenden), 9, 10, 188
Primary schools, 31
Private schools, 19, 20, 21, 25; alumni, monies of, 28; class snobbery, 28, 29; competition, 22, 23, 24, 25; diversity, 24; IQ tests, 26; meritocracy, notion of, 22, 24; minorities, 24; social status, 25
Professing Feminism, 182
Public Agenda, 12
Public schools, and discipline, 73

Index

Puff Daddy, 92
Putnam County (N.Y.), 103

Raising Cain: Protecting the Emotional Life of Boys (Thompson and Kindlon), 95, 96
Ready to Learn, 52
Reich, Charles, 157
"Revisiting the Mommy Track" (*Newsweek*), 11
Revolution from Within (Steinem), 131
Rieff, Phillip, 55, 130
Rimes, LeAnn, 87
Riverdale (private school), 21
Rivers, Caryl, 184
Rockdale County (Ga.), xvi, 110, 117, 118, 119
Rocket Man, 91
Rodberg, Simon, 166, 168
Roffman, Deborah M., 129
Roiphe, Katie, 173
Romper Room, 48
Root, Barbara, 25, 32
Rosensweig, Nora, 74
Rubin, Lillian, 131, 136
Russell Sage Foundation, 50
Rutgers University, 140, 141, 142, 145

Sacred Heart (private school), 21, 25, 32
Safe sex, 130
St. Ann's (private school), 21, 23
St. Bernard's (private school), 21, 22, 25
Saint Charles (Mo.), 78
Salon, 7, 18, 186
San Francisco, 150, 151, 152
SAS Institute, 159
Saturday Night Fever, 23
Saturday Night Live, 38
Saylor, Michael, 164

Scarsdale (N.Y.), 24
School discipline, 73, 74, 80, 81; erosion of, 79; lawsuits, fear of, 80; moral values, 81, 82
School principals, 83, 84
School safety, 79, 80, 81, 83; and bullies, 84; and teachers, 85
Schumer, Charles, 29
Schwartz, Felice, 9
Scientific rationalism, 124
Score!, 161
Scream, 92
"Second Step," 81
Seinfeld, Jerry, 123
Seinfeld, 123
Self-employment, 159
Sesame Street, xiii, 35; American anti-intellectualism, embracing of, 39, 40, 41, 53; celebrities, obsession with, 38; commercialization of, 52, 53; criticism of, 43, 44; diversity, 39; effects of, 50, 51, 52; glibness of, 45, 46; history of, 36, 37, 46, 47, 48; and literacy, 51, 52, 53; popularity of, reasons for, 49, 50; purpose of, 40–41
Seventeen, 130
Sex: masturbation, 134; mechanics, reduced to, 128; medicalization of, 127, 130; morality, 131; mystery of, 128; and personal identity, 132, 133; promiscuity, 133; sadomasochism, 135, 136
Sex and the City, 177
Sex education, xvii, 127, 128, 129
Sexual liberation, xvii
Shopping Mall High School, 141
Shopping Mall University, 141
Shopping-mall curriculum. *See* College.
Sidel, Ruth, 15
Silicon Alley Reporter, 155

Index

Silicon Valley, 151, 163
Simon, Paul, 38
Simpson, Bart, 98
Simpson, O. J., 135
Simpsons, The, 46, 112
Sims, Lottie, 90
Sinatra, Frank, 92
Single mothers, 12
Singles, 123, 131
Singular Generation, The
    (Urbanska), 122
Smeal, Eleanor, 170
Smiley, Guy, 42
Smith, Will, 92
Smith College, 140
Smithsonian Institution, 35
Social Register, The, 25
Solomon, T. J., 117
Sparks.com, 152, 164, 165, 166,
    167
Special education, 75; and
    juvenile criminality, 75
Spence (private school), 21, 22,
    25, 30
Spice Girls, 105, 107
Spock, Dr. Benjamin, xv, 56, 57,
    63, 64
Sports Illustrated for Kids, 92
Spur Posse, 137
Spy in the House of Love, A
    (Nin), 133
Stability and Change in Human
    Characteristics (Bloom), 47
Star Trek, 37
State University of New York at
    Albany, 142
Stearns, Peter, xvii, 59, 124, 126
Steelcase, 154
Steinem, Gloria, 9, 131, 132,
    180, 182
Stendhal, 122, 134
Streep, Meryl, 38
Students: and due process, 77,
    79; free-speech, 76, 77, 78,
    79; sexual harassment, 82
Supreme Court, 76, 77, 82

Survivor, 20, 23, 29, 31
Sweeney, Jennifer Foote, 18, 186
Sylvan Centers, 161
Syphilis, and teenagers, 110. *See*
    also "Lost Children of
    Rockdale County, The."

Taliban, 170
"Talking with Kids About Tough
    Issues," 113
Temple Emanu-El, 22
Thompson, Michael, 95, 96
Thoreau, Henry David, 148
Three Stooges, The, 47
Time, 8, 69, 109, 117, 118, 119,
    120, 163, 178, 184
Time Bind, The (Hochschild),
    154
Tinker v. Des Moines School
    District, 76, 78, 79
Tinkerbell Company, 91
Titanic, 92, 106
Tocqueville, Alexis de, 67
Toddlers and Parents (Brazelton),
    58
Tomlin, Lily, 38, 46
"Tortoise and the Hare, The,"
    45
Towne (private school), 21
Toy Manufacturers Association
    of America, 160
Toy Manufacturers of America
    Factbook, 89
Toys, as learning tools, 160, 161
A Traveler from Altruria
    (Howells), 157
Trevor, Henry, 88, 93
Trevor Day (private school), 21
Tribe Apart, A (Hersch), 100
Trilling, Lionel, 124
Trinity (private school), 21
Tutoring, 26, 27
Twain, Mark, 109
TWBA/Chiat/Day advertising,
    160

A NOTE ON THE AUTHOR

Kay S. Hymowitz is a senior fellow at The Manhattan Institute in New York City and a contributing editor of *City Journal*. Born in Philadelphia, she studied at Brandeis, Tufts, and Columbia universities; before turning to writing full time, she taught English literature and composition at Brooklyn College and the Parsons School of Design. Ms. Hymowitz has written extensively on education and childhood in America, in articles for the *New York Times*, the *Washington Post*, the *Wall Street Journal*, the *New Republic*, the *Public Interest*, *Commentary*, *Dissent*, and *Tikkun*, among other publications. She is also the author of *Ready or Not: Why Treating Our Children as Small Adults Endangers Their Future and Ours*. She lives in Brooklyn with her husband and three children.